churchmorph

how megatrends are
reshaping christian communities

eddie gibbs

Baker Academic

a division of Baker Publishing Group
Grand Rapids, Michigan

© 2009 by Eddie Gibbs

Published by Baker Academic
a division of Baker Publishing Group
P.O. Box 6287, Grand Rapids, MI 49516–6287
www.bakeracademic.com

Printed in the United States of America

Library of Congress Cataloging-in-Publication Data
Gibbs, Eddie.
    ChurchMorph : how megatrends are reshaping Christian communities / Eddie
Gibbs.
        p.   cm.
    Includes bibliographical references and index.
    ISBN 978-0-8010-3762-7 (pbk.)
        1. Church renewal. 2. Church growth. 3. Communities—Religious aspects—
Christianity. 4. Postmodernism—Religious aspects—Christianity. I. Title.
    BV600.3.G527 2009
    270.8′3—dc22   2009009314

contents

series preface

Allelon is a network of missional church leaders, schools, and parachurch organizations that inspires, engages, trains, educates, and provides resources to leaders working to fulfill the church's mission in our culture. Simply put, together we are a movement of missional leaders.

We want, in particular, to serve those who are involved in new forms of missional communities (sometimes called "emerging"), those starting new congregations within denominational systems, and those in existing congregations who are working toward missional identity and engagement. Our desire is to encourage, support, coach, and offer companionship for missional leaders as they discern new models of church capable of sustaining a living and faithful witness to the gospel in our contemporary world.

The word *allelon* is a common but overlooked Greek word that is reciprocal in nature. In the New Testament it is most often translated "one another." Christian faith is not an individual matter. Everything in the life of the church is done *allelon*, for the sake of the world. A Christian community is defined by the *allelon* sayings in Scripture: love one another, pursue one another's good, build up one another.

The overarching mission of Allelon is to educate and encourage the church, learning from one another so that we might become a people among whom God lives, a people whose lives are a sign, symbol, and foretaste of God's redeeming love in neighborhoods and in the whole of society. We seek to facilitate this reality among ordinary women and men who endeavor to participate in God's mission to reclaim and restore all of creation, bearing witness to the world of a new way of being human.

To help accomplish this goal, Allelon has partnered with Baker Books and Baker Academic to produce resources that equip the church in thinking about and practicing missional life. We are excited to promote Eddie Gibbs's book as it identifies the various trends and changes within the church in our context today. Eddie has been a wise mentor and an observer of the church for decades, and on the basis of this experience he keenly reveals some of the radical experiments that are being undertaken in the life of the church. He is a blessing to the church, and this book will help spur God's people on into new and additional experiments as we seek to bear witness to God's redemptive life.

Mark Priddy
CEO, Allelon International
www.allelon.org

introduction

In the course of teaching and mentoring in the School of Intercultural Studies at Fuller Theological Seminary for the past two decades, I have been deluged with books describing and critiquing persistent trends in churches throughout the Western world. These changes are evident in churches and renewal and evangelistic movements across the theological spectrum and within many traditions.

After forty-five years of professional ministry and years of reflecting on the many movements that have embodied church renewal, I feel that the time has come to step back and review the current picture, recognizing its intriguing complexity. At the outset, I acknowledge that this is an ambitious project to attempt within the pages of a short book and with my limited resources. Nevertheless, because of the convergence of a number of factors that I will address in the course of identifying the external and internal movements for change in the first two chapters, I believe an attempt is warranted and timely.

My purpose in writing is, in the first place, to inform and encourage by providing a representative, but by no means exhaustive, survey. Second, it is to offer an interpretive commentary on the most significant developments in various streams of church life in the Western world. It is important to appreciate just how extensive and complex are the changes represented by the missional church discussions, the emerging church phenomenon, the transitions taking place within some high-profile megachurches, various expressions of indigenous missional communities reaching out to the multifaceted urban cultural mosaic, and the resurgent Reformed network that is attracting a significant number of younger evangelicals. Many readers may be familiar with part of this picture, and as active participants may in fact be more knowledgeable than the author, but they may also be so immersed as to not have the benefit of being able to stand back and observe the overarching trends.

Recent retirement from a heavy teaching and mentoring load has provided me with the opportunity, between speaking engagements, to explore numerous Web sites and blogs, both to extend and to update my own awareness of current trends. The younger, tech-savvy generation certainly exhibits a high standard in terms of presentation and technical sophistication! I hope that readers will take time to sample some of the online sources that are cited. In addition to gathering information from numerous Web sites, I have had the opportunity to visit a few of the locations that are mentioned here, and I am privileged both to know some of the leaders personally and to consult occasionally with a number of them.

Having completed the first draft, I sought the wisdom of a range of leaders who could provide further insight and correct any errors they found there. I am especially grateful to the following people, who reviewed either the entire manuscript or sections that related to their own sphere of ministry: Brian Auten, Ryan Bolger, Peter Brierley, Wayne Gordon, Alan Hirsch, Cam Roxburgh, Bill White, and J. R. Woodward. I have benefited enormously from their insights and incorporated many of their suggestions.

This book is intended for two categories of readers. It is for people, like myself, who struggle to assess the extent and overall significance of current ecclesial trends, or who are worried about such trends, based upon the critiques of scholars and church leaders. It is also intended for leaders who are immersed in one of the streams to such an extent that they have little opportunity to view the bigger picture.

I share some of the concerns voiced by critics of emerging and missional thinking. However, we cannot be prematurely dismissive, because many of the issues being raised are deeply significant for the ongoing mission of the church in the West. We must not lose sight of the bigger picture—the need to reenvision a church that is significantly different from the church that has been shaped and subverted by modernity and the culture of Christendom. Churches in the West need to be motivated and shaped by a missional commitment to a pluralistic world floundering in a sea of relativism.

I believe that the trends identified in chapters 3 through 8 provide signs of the kingdom, reflecting how different ecclesial communities are redefining "church" in a post-Christendom environment. Within a changing cultural milieu the church will always exist as the "becoming church." Within the relatively limited compass of this book, I attempt to provide a survey, with samples by way of illustration. Although it does not claim to be comprehensive, I trust that the range of examples will be sufficient to provide encouragement and assurance that the Lord has by no means abandoned his church, but rather that in these days God is "up to something" significant.

In the midst of upheaval and reconfiguration, it is important to ensure that we continue to seek fresh insight from Scripture and that our search for contextualization represents a radical obedience to the gospel within specific cultural contexts, and not a sellout to culture. Time alone will tell which expressions of church will prove to be passing fads and which will establish strategic frontiers. Across the board, open, honest criticism and accountability are necessary for the health and vitality of churches as they morph, experiencing transformation through the process of engaging in mission. While the fundamental nature of the church remains as the body and bride of Christ, its forms will change and fluctuate through time and according to context.

In sending this manuscript to the publishers I am acutely aware of its limitations. It is a daunting task to attempt such a broad-based survey. Furthermore, as with any significant movement that is largely decentralized, the scenario is in constant flux. Between the time of signing off and eventual publication, further developments will have occurred. Perhaps some of the examples described will no longer exist or will have morphed out of recognition, and there will be yet new developments that will need to be identified and assessed. Such is the dynamic nature of the church in all its exhilarating and perplexing variety, as the risen Christ continues to build his church until the day of its completion on his return.

Finally I would like to express my appreciation to Robert Hosack at Baker Academic for suggesting this project and my indebtedness to managing editor Brian Bolger and his team for their diligence and patience through the editorial process and guidance through the Web site jungle.

Eddie Gibbs
Pasadena, 2008

— 1 —

megatrends convulsing the western world

For the past seven years the focus of my concern for the church has broadened from a preoccupation with internal, institutional factors that contribute to the vitality of the church to embrace an interest in the changing contexts in which the church finds itself and the challenges these contexts present to leadership. The economic, technological, and social changes taking place throughout Western societies are so comprehensive and traumatic that all institutions become embroiled. Even churches are inevitably caught up in their wake. They may persist in denying that such widespread changes are actually occurring. They may attempt to minimize their significance. Or they may try to craft strategies, in an attempt to insulate themselves from the effects of such convulsions. But, sooner or later, they will not be able to escape their impact.

Indeed, inherited denominations continue to experience, almost without exception, the unrelenting decline in both membership and attendance that began in North America during the mid-1960s.[1]

The fact that churches representing different ecclesial structures and theological positions are encountering the same challenges at the same time indicates that there are deep-level and widespread issues that need to be identified and addressed. The range of issues is both contextual and systemic in nature and cannot be adequately addressed simply by tweaking here and there, by adding programs, reworking the organizational structures, or attempting to improve internal communications to fix specific problems.

The organizational structures of historic churches were designed for a different cultural context, in which change was more predictable and occurred at a slower pace. Today, we live in a culture of discontinuous and often unpredictable change. When things happen suddenly and unexpectedly, the church needs organizational structures that are flexible and flat—that is, capable of adjusting to changing needs and circumstances to allow for timely and appropriate responses. This is a challenge faced by every institution, including those within business, politics, education, health care, and the military, as well as the church.

Hierarchical structures are increasingly problematic, because decision making has to go through a chain of command and levels of control. Individuals find themselves boxed into the structure, every person according to their level and within their department. Vertical relationships are emphasized at the expense of horizontal engagement. This compartmentalization contributes to an ongoing competition for resources between areas of ministry and staff persons who champion their own causes, lacking a clear picture of and strong commitment to the broader mission and agenda of the church. Hierarchies paralyze initiative and are ponderous in responding to unanticipated challenges.

The decline within traditional denominations has been, in some measure, compensated for by the proliferation of megachurches. Many of these churches are relational in ethos while controlling in governance. Some of these churches are independent, while a significant number are affiliated with a parent denomination—although it must be said that they tend to have much more in common with other evangelical or Pentecostal churches of their size and influence than they do with the churches of their own theological and ecclesial traditions.

Indeed, the current church scene in North America, and to a lesser extent in Europe and Australasia, may be more accurately described as "post-denominational." This term does not imply the extinction of denominations as discrete entities, but rather the demise of what might be called their "tribal" insularity. They share insights and draw strength from each other, rather than depend upon denominational programs and resources.

For the past few decades a number of movements have brought churches together from different denominations, networks, and independent congregations. Such movements include the charismatic movement; youth movements such as Young Life, Youth for Christ, and more recently, Soul Survivor (an organization that began in the United Kingdom and is now also active in the United States); as well as campus-based ministries like InterVarsity Fellowship (Universities and Colleges Christian Fellowship in the United Kingdom) and Campus Crusade. During the 1980s and early '90s, the church growth movement also brought together large numbers of pastors from a wide range of traditions to address issues surrounding leadership and church management. Lastly, we must mention the impact of the Willow Creek Association and the pastors' conferences hosted by Saddleback Community Church, along with the Alpha course, the evangelistic program created by Holy Trinity Brompton in West London. These three forums have catapulted Bill Hybels, Rick Warren, and Nicky Gumbel onto a pan-denominational, international stage and sphere of influence.

Christianity's Image Taking a Turn for the Worse

In 2007, David Kinnaman, president of the Barna Research group, together with Gabe Lyons of the Fermi Project, a collaborative group that works to relate faith to the broader culture, authored a book entitled *unChristian*. In it, they presented some disturbing findings on "what a new generation really thinks about Christianity." *UnChristian* highlights Christianity's tarnished image and declining influence in the United States, particularly among sixteen- to twenty-nine-year-olds. A decade ago, an overwhelming majority of non-Christians, including those in that age category, were "favorably" disposed toward Christianity's role in society. But today just 16 percent of non-Christians in that age bracket have a "good impression" of Christianity. In the study, evangelical Christians come under the severest attack, with just 3 percent of sixteen- to twenty-nine-year-old non-Christians indicating favorable views toward this subgroup of believers.[2]

Kinnaman and Lyons found that the most common perceptions held by young non-Christians about American Christianity were that it is anti-homosexual (91 percent), judgmental (87 percent), hypocritical (85 percent), old-fashioned (78 percent), too involved in politics (75 percent), boring (68 percent), not accepting of other faiths (64 percent), and insensitive to others (70 percent).[3] Strikingly, half of young Christian believers surveyed for *unChristian* viewed their religion in the very same way: too judgmental, hypocritical, and overly politicized.[4] One-third said it was old-fashioned and out of touch with reality. The study also found that many Christians were aware of their religion's image problem. More than one in ten evangelicals believe that Americans are becoming more hostile and negative toward Christianity.

Theologically conservative Christians are widely perceived as being aloof and unwilling to engage in genuine dialogue, out of fear of "caving in" to the broader culture. But such openness is essential in relating to Mosaics (known also as "Generation Y") and Busters (known also as "Generation X"), who represent the "conversation generations." According to Kinnaman and Lyons,

> Mosaics and Busters . . . want to discuss, debate, and question everything. This can be either a source of frustration or an interest we use to facilitate new and lasting levels of spiritual depth in young people. Young outsiders want to have discussion, but they perceive Christians as unwilling to engage in genuine dialogue. They think of conversations as "persuasion" sessions, in which the Christian downloads as many arguments as possible.[5]

Kinnaman and Lyons also show that although the world of young people is inundated with choices related to media, movies, television, and technology, most churchgoing teens report that they rarely recall learning anything helpful on these topics in church. This attitude reveals a serious disconnect between the church's agenda and young people's preoccupations. Perhaps the biggest disconnect was the perception they had of the lack of genuineness in care and sincerity displayed by evangelicals when evangelizing non-Christians.

While the church's agenda need not be driven by the preoccupations of young people, especially the issues involving popular culture, the church does, however, need to endeavor to understand these issues and address them in an empathetic and discerning manner, knowing when to affirm and when to confront. Contextualization, properly applied, does not imply selling out to culture but rather demonstrating the complex relationship that the gospel has to any culture, as evidenced in the New Testament itself. The followers of Christ engaged first the Jewish worldview, and then the Greco-Roman cultural contexts.

Across ecclesial and theological traditions, the current situation is in a state of flux. Not only are churchgoers shopping around from church to church, but they also demonstrate an eclectic spirituality. Many evangelicals are shifting between liturgical and contemporary expressions of worship, moving from one to the other (and sometimes back again). Among the "emerging adult" generation (ages eighteen to thirty-five), there are those who are walking away from the evangelicalism in which they were nurtured as children, perceiving it as too rationalistic or intellectually impoverished. This represents an acceleration of the "Evangelicals on the Canterbury Trail" phenomenon that began at Wheaton College in the late 1980s under the influence of the late Robert Webber. At the same time, there is within the same age bracket a resurgent Reformed movement, which offers theological coherence along with a call to intellectual commitment and spiritual vitality.[6]

While the churchgoing population in the United States is still large enough to mask the extent of the unreached and alienated segment of the population, in Europe the scene is drastically different. The vast majority of Europe's population is disconnected from church life. The long established cultural/religious rites of passage, such as baptisms, weddings, and funerals, are fading in significance. It must be admitted that, for the most part, if a church in Europe is experiencing significant growth, it is doing so mainly at the expense of other local churches. And those same churches, if they are reaching out to the unchurched to any significant extent, are generally only gathering in those who have more recently ceased to be involved with a church; they are making little impact on those who, because of past hurts or general skepticism about the church's relevance to their lives, are resistant to institutional religion.

Potential for numerical growth is not an issue of church size or new program development. Both large and small churches can trumpet their particular merits. Some people prefer a church that is large enough to offer a comprehensive range of worship experiences and programs, much like a department store offers one-stop shopping. Other churchgoers, however, prefer the "boutique" store environment, where the experience and atmosphere are tailor-made to their particular tastes and where an intimate atmosphere pervades. Unlike the experience of many who attend a big church, you cannot get lost or go unnoticed in a congregation with under one hundred worshipers in attendance—at least, that is what long-time members of smaller churches like to think. But both of these experiences, whether large or small church, are couched in consumer terms, and therein lies the problem and the challenge.

The Process of Morphing

The "morphing" of the church relates to its transitioning to a new identity as a missional presence in the West. There is a growing realization among leaders committed to mission that the challenge will not be adequately met by adding new programs to ensure the local church's—or a denomination's—institutional survival. Such leaders are talking about an unfettered reimagining of the church, resulting in a comprehensive change in its self-understanding and its configuration.

The term "deconstruction" is frequently used by radical voices within the emergent church. But this technical term is often misunderstood, being perceived as too threatening and confrontational. It is heard to imply demolition and destruction, which is not what is intended. Deconstruction instead describes a particular method of literary criticism that seeks to get behind the text to reveal the embedded assumptions. Among emerging church leaders, deconstruction signifies not destruction, but a breakthrough. It means to undo or take apart in order to arrive at a deeper understanding, allowing for a creative rereading.[7] However, in order to avoid the negative implications of the term, and its highly technical explanation, I prefer to speak of the "reimagining" of the church, and of the transformation process as the "morphing" of the church.

Wikipedia defines "morphing" as a special effect in motion pictures and animations that changes (or morphs) one image into another through a seamless transition. The term has a much more ancient usage however. It is derived from the Greek word *morphe*, which appears in the New Testament in a significant context. The apostle Paul writes to the Philippians,

> Let the same mind be in you that was in Christ Jesus,
> who, though he was in the form [*morphe*] of God,
>   did not regard equality with God
>   as something to be exploited,
> but emptied himself,
>   taking the form [*morphe*] of a slave,
>   being born in human likeness.
> And being found in human form,
>   he humbled himself
>   and became obedient to the point of death—
>   even death on a cross.
>
>   Philippians 2:5–8 (NRSV)

Gordon Fee explains the meaning of *morphe* in the following terms: "Since *morphe* can denote 'form' or 'shape' in terms of both the external features by which something is recognized and the characteristics and qualities that are essential to it, it was precisely the right word to characterize both the reality (his being God) and the metaphor (his taking on the role of a slave)."[8] The mission on which Jesus embarked necessitated a radical transition from sovereign Lord to humble servant. It entailed his abandoning of heaven in order to live among sinful humankind, with all the limitations of a bodily existence. While the morphing of the church is of a different order, it too must be prepared to undergo costly, radical, and comprehensive changes in the process of dying to itself, in submission to Christ's will.

What does such a transition signify for the church, and why is it necessary? As we have noted, the inherited denominations are all in serious decline. Growing churches, whether denominational or independent, are bucking the trend largely as a result of transfer growth or, to a lesser extent, through the renewed participation of the lapsed. The widespread nature of decline across the ecclesial and theological spectrum and over the same time span indicates that the root causes of the slump are not primarily within the life of religious institutions. Rather, they relate to broader issues arising from their cultural context. Such changes are not restricted to local circumstances but arise from the cultural turbulence that is convulsing the entire Western world. The morphing of the church describes the process of transformation of the church as it was, or as it exists today, to the church as it needs to become in order to engage appropriately and significantly in God's mission in the context of the twenty-first century.

Some might argue that reimagination is not the problem and that churches should instead focus on a whole-hearted application of the scriptural understanding of the church as the people of God gathered, preaching the Word, sharing the gospel, making disciples of all peoples, taking care of widows and orphans, and otherwise fulfilling its intended purpose in the world. Application *is* precisely the issue, but this has to be undertaken in changing contexts, which present unfamiliar challenges to most Western churches. In a post-Christendom and pluralist environment, the Christian church is no longer in a privileged position, but is one of a number of competing entities. It is operating among people who, for the most part, do not have a biblical awareness of the story of redemption, the life and mission of Jesus Christ, or the nature and scope of the good news that Christ proclaimed.

Sadly, this lack of awareness is prevalent even among the church-going population, many of whom also fail to grasp that the risen Lord commissioned his followers to share his message of good news throughout the world. Consequently, application cannot be undertaken on the basis of assumptions drawn from previous experience, but rather requires a prayerful reimagination. Only by so doing will the people with whom we seek to communicate be able to hear the timeless message of the gospel in a timely manner. They need to encounter God addressing them in the here and now, rather than in some remote time and place.

A Missional Response to Megatrends

There are five megatrends impacting the churches of the West. These are the transition from modernity to postmodernity; the transition from the industrial to the information age; the transition from Christendom to post-Christendom contexts; the transition from production initiatives to consumer awareness; and the transition from religious identity to spiritual exploration. We will now unpack each of these transitions in order to appreciate their significance for the life and witness of the church.

From Modernity to Postmodernity

Modernity represents the period of time during which traditional societal structures, in which authority was invested in hierarchies historically represented by the church and the state, or, where monarchy prevailed, by the crown, transitioned into new forms. Prior to this time, the authority of prelates and princes could be questioned only at the peril of those who begged to differ and dared to mount a challenge. Increasingly, this authority structure was challenged by modernity, which was birthed among independent scholars and artists in the universities. They were the product of the Renaissance, which arose in Italy and France in the fourteenth and fifteenth centuries and flourished into the seventeenth century, and were marked by their celebration of the human capacity for reasoning and artistic creativity. On the heels of the Renaissance, the Enlightenment arose in the seventeenth and eighteenth centuries, fostering an intellectual climate of free thinking, especially in regard to philosophical and theological reasoning and political innovation.

These two movements released vast resources of human potential, which had largely remained dormant under the oppressive climate of pre-modern societies. They restored a measure of respect for the biblical story of creation, emphasizing that humans are made in the image of God and, therefore, are endowed with the creative urges of their Creator. Consequently, the seventeenth and eighteenth centuries heralded unprecedented scientific and technological progress, and this age of inquiry and innovation continued to unfold as the following two centuries witnessed undreamed of progress in the areas of medicine, transportation, and communication, to name but a few. Unfortunately, humankind eventually became intoxicated by its own sense of progress. Confidence inflated into arrogance.

Then came the growing realization that we had, at the same time, unleashed destructive powers, even more potent than our creative genius. We have witnessed and been embroiled in the indiscriminate mass destruction caused by modern warfare. We are only now belatedly waking up to the environmental consequences of our reckless disregard for the finely balanced ecosystems that sustain this planet, and we are beginning to question the sustainability of our consumer-driven society. We are suffering, in increasing measure, the social consequences of our rootless and fragmented lives, in which striving for more is never enough but rather stimulates further dissatisfaction. An increased standard of living does not signify an enhanced quality of life.[9]

Postmodernity represents a comprehensive questioning of the facile assumptions of modernity. In addition to reassessing the past, it is increasingly uncertain and fearful of the future. We live in a cultural context of heightened levels of anxiety. We despair of how to go about planning for an uncertain future, so instead we resort to hunkering down and finding contentment in living from day to day.

Postmodernity presents a missional challenge to the Protestant churches and the evangelical movements that arose in Europe and North America during the era of modernity. Some of these movements go back to the sixteenth-century Reformation in Europe, while others are the product of nineteenth-century Revivalism in

North America. Each became tainted by rationalistic approaches designed to defend the inspiration and authority of Scripture and, among many evangelicals, by the self-confident assumption that strategies and plans can be devised to fulfill within this generation the missionary mandate to take the gospel to the entire world. This is not to overlook the parallel emphases of personal holiness and intercessory prayer as vital contributing factors. But such acknowledgment of our dependency on God's initiatives and the power of the Holy Spirit was often regarded as being part of a cause-and-effect relationship: intercessory prayer was the instrument and revival the consequence. However, such a line of reasoning fails to make the logical distinction between correlation and causation. The presence of the former does not guarantee the latter outcome.

As Protestant and evangelical churches morph from modernity to postmodernity, this process will entail the reinstatement of a sense of mystery in our worship, as was evident in premodern times; yet now the mystery can be embraced without the superstition that then prevailed. It will also require that churches become more self-critical, rather than maintaining a denial-based assertiveness. Churches will need to recognize and confess how they were subverted more than they realized by the assumptions of modernity. It is our planning based on rationalistic assumptions, together with our stage-managed and celebrity-focused worship, that have driven away many in the "delayed adulthood" category. They have abandoned program-driven churches in search of a more authentic spirituality.

From the Industrial Age to the Information Age

The Renaissance and the Enlightenment contributed to the end of the monopolistic position of the Roman Catholic church in the West. The rise of modern nation-states brought about a decentralization of power. The Reformation, both in mainland Europe and in the United Kingdom, resulted in the creation of autonomous national churches. At first they struggled, when challenged by new religious movements seeking their independence on a number of theological and ecclesial issues, to maintain their exclusive position. Eventually the church within the nation fragmented into a variety of

competing denominations, which matched the competitive capitalism that generated the wealth and ingenuity that fed an expanding
consumerism.

The late eighteenth century gave birth to the Industrial Revolution,
which developed rapidly in the following centuries. It profoundly
impacted every area of life, including agriculture, manufacturing,
transportation, and living conditions. It ushered in waves of vast
internal migration, as people moved from the country to the new
industrial centers in order to work in the coal mines, foundries, and
factories. These industrial centers served as magnets to the surrounding rural population. In the United States, the Civil War provided
the catalyst for rapid industrial expansion. Then two world wars
created demand for mass production on an unprecedented scale.
In response, the first half of the twentieth century witnessed the
emergence of huge manufacturing plants and centrally organized
distribution networks.

The entrepreneurship of capitalism found its most dynamic expression in North America. This dynamism was not confined to the
business and industrial worlds. It also created a "can-do" climate
in the church that witnessed the birth of scores of denominations
and hundreds of independent religious movements. These continue
to proliferate even today. Thus Protestantism in general and evangelicalism in particular were shaped and stimulated by the spirit
of competitive capitalism. They were the religious equivalent of
"big business," operating with the same hierarchical structures and
controlling leadership style. However, there were some significant
exceptions, such as the Congregationalists and Baptists.

The great majority of churches today are led by the Builder or
Boomer generations, which represent, respectively, the elitist control
and delegated leadership paradigm. The difference between the two
generations lies in their style rather than in their substance. Build-
ers tend to be more aloof, whereas Boomers are more relational.
These are generalizations with many exceptions, but as broad categories they helpfully describe the climate and culture of so many
churches.

Churches shaped by the big-business models of the industrial age,
with their centralization of power and dependent and accountable

branch offices, struggled to interpret the different entrepreneurial climate of the information age. The most dysfunctional among them are those denominations that trace their history to the state churches of Europe. Their structures are the most hierarchical and ponderous. The challenges they face parallel those of major corporations when their markets became increasingly diversified and subject to sudden changes in customer demands. Whereas denominational executives find themselves too removed from the frontline and overwhelmed by institutional challenges, preoccupied with "firefighting" flare-ups and with downsizing strategies, it is those church leaders at ground level, grappling with the challenges of ministry and mission in their local contexts, who are most aware of the changes taking place.

The exponential spread of the Internet and development of powerful search engines ushered in the information age. The democratization of knowledge has undermined the power positions of elitist leaders who previously held the monopoly on information. They are no longer the gatekeepers, allowing only approved individuals and groups access to information. Leadership no longer consists exclusively of those individuals who are "in the know" because they had been privileged by top management, on whom they continue to be dependent. No longer is patronage a powerful instrument of control. The new generation of leaders represents those who have street-level credibility and "know-how" to mentor and empower those they recruited and those with whom they work. They also understand how to operate within an expanding network, distinguishing between and separating out influence from control.

The morphing of the church relates both to inherited denominations and to megachurches. If the latter carry a denominational label, they operate with a fair degree of independence, functioning much like a mini-denomination, and at times exercising more influence than their collective parent body. Morphing also relates to those contemporary networks of churches that have imbibed more of the control mechanism of the industrial age.

What then will morphing entail as churches transition from the industrial age to the information age? It will require a flattening of structures to ensure flexible and prompt responses to rapidly changing conditions. It will also mean recognizing that most significant innovation and new, supportive, risk-taking networks will arise at the local level and from the margins, rather than from the center and from the top down.

Hierarchical leaders, for their part, must release themselves from their organizational entrapment in order to observe firsthand what is happening at every level of church life, and to keep in close touch with the innovators. They must become the permission-givers, even while insisting on accountability. Denominational leaders do not like being surprised, so they must be kept fully informed. But this does not necessarily entail asking for permission! Ground-level innovators may have to work outside of their denomination's conceptual and organizational box. If they ask for permission, their request may be declined due to organizational constraints. The key is to establish a relationship of trust and to work with wise mentors.

As ground-level initiatives prosper, critics will arise to complain to the leadership of the denomination. That is why two-way communication channels and accountability structures are so important. They enable leaders to hear directly from those who are taking these missional initiatives rather than only from their critics. Those held responsible within the denominational hierarchy need to be able to respond to critics by saying that they are in direct contact with the individuals concerned and are kept fully informed. Only then can they serve as advocates of those innovators under critical review.

The morphing of the church also means that information is widely available throughout the fellowship of believers. Each person within every local congregation plays an active role and is taken into confidence as a friend. Such widespread communication works best in a small church, or in a large church broken down into smaller units, each of which enjoys a measure of independence that fosters initiative-taking.

From the Christendom Era to Post-Christendom Contexts

For the first 250 years of its life, the church operated from the margins of society. It was either barely tolerated or actively persecuted. Frequently it was misunderstood and misrepresented. A monumental effort was required in order to shift the tide of public opinion. This came about because of the distinctive lifestyle of the early Christians, their impact on society, and their increasing influence due to their exponential growth. We see a dynamic movement that was not reliant on real estate; neither did it depend on academic training institutions to provide leadership. It was a ground-level, popular movement that turned upside down the world of its day, so much so that by early in the fourth century, the Roman emperor Constantine came to the conclusion that if he could not beat them, he had better join them! So was born what we have come to know as Christendom, which lasted for the next sixteen hundred years in the Western world.

Under Christendom, the church was granted a privileged position as an agent of the state. It provided the moral and ideological bulwark of society. Especially in the European context, and to a lesser extent in North America, the inherited denominations represented churches one was born into, rather than churches one could elect to join. Priests and pastors served as chaplains to the majority of the community, instead of being restricted to the gathered congregation. But as Christendom gave way to a secular and religiously pluralistic society, so the ministry sphere of priests and pastors began to shrink.

The major challenge facing Christendom-era churches was the activation of their nominal and marginal members, who made up an extensive external constituency. But with the advent of post-Christendom social contexts during the twentieth century, church attendance shrank as people became increasingly socially distanced from the life of the church. In North America especially, people tend to drop out of church when they move to areas of the country where the church tradition in which they were nurtured from childhood is no longer a dominant influence.

Churches with a parochial mentality operate on a "come-to-us" philosophy of ministry. Newcomers will be welcomed, but they will be expected to take the initiative in stepping through the doorway of the church. Here in the United States, the same strategy prevails among megachurches and independent smaller churches. Provided they can demonstrate greater relevance, develop a range of need-meeting ministries, and advertise their presence, they can attract the free-floating religious seekers who have become dissatisfied with their present brand, or local expression, of church.

For the church to morph into a post-Christendom context, it will need to adopt a different approach to ministry—from attraction to incarnational presence in the community. The Christian church is no longer in a privileged position in the culture, so it must learn to operate from the margins, much like the early church. Yet, the West presents an even greater religious challenge, for in the eyes of many people today the church has been tried and found wanting. In this new context churches will have to reestablish both their credibility, in order to demonstrate the radical nature of the gospel, and their transforming impact on society.

The process of morphing will be prolonged and painful for those churches that have a long history of enjoying Christendom privileges and prestige and that are steeped in a venerable tradition. The growing megachurches face a different but no less daunting challenge. Their recent success could prove to be their greatest downfall, should they fail to recognize the complexity of the cultural changes that are taking place. They must ignore the loud voices that proclaim, "If it's not broke, why fix it?"

Despite the pressures to continue business as usual, a tide of change is surging through the churches of the Western world. This tidal flow has traveled further and faster in Europe, where Christendom functionally collapsed from about the time of the First World War, a war that had such a devastating impact in terms of the loss of millions of lives on the Western Front and the destruction of cities in Europe. The devastation was repeated on a much greater scale with the bombing of cities in the Second World War. Christendom may still survive as state pageantry and ecclesiastical pretensions to grandeur, but under the façade, society is increasingly anti-Christian, or at least demonstrates an ever-lower tolerance level.

In the United States, the Christendom paradigm took on a different form, due to the separation of church and state and the proliferation of both denominational and independent congregations. At the national level it appears as a vaguely defined deistic, civil religion, enhanced by a resurrected belief in "manifest destiny." Much is made of the country's Judeo-Christian heritage, which is increasingly challenged by those of other faiths, as well as by increasing numbers of people declaring no religious preference, bolstered by the vocal minority of atheists.

From Production Initiatives to Consumer Awareness

The United States has led the world in both its technological innovations and its scale of production. Its genius for innovations in manufacturing became evident by the middle of the nineteenth century. At that time, American manufacturers moved beyond a craftsman approach, which entailed making each item separately with the result that individual parts could not be interchanged, to an assembly line concept, which meant producing standardized parts that were then assembled into the final product.

Henry Ford developed the assembly line concept for the mass production of automobiles, which brought down their price to the extent that the automobile was no longer the status symbol of the rich but was within the reach of the average American family. Factories churned out an unprecedented volume of reliable products to meet the overwhelming demand for transportation, armaments, and a wide range of goods during two world wars. Constant updates were introduced to keep pace with rapidly developing technologies and the need to meet and surpass the performance of the enemy.

Whereas Europe and Japan lay devastated and exhausted following World War II, the cities of the United States remained intact and its industrial base unharmed. Manufacturers in these cities were poised to take advantage of global needs, with the transition from war production to the task of rebuilding and resupplying devastated cities. The United States' industrialists knew how to produce high quality goods in great quantity. The two decades from 1946 to 1966 were decades of unprecedented peacetime mass production.

By the mid-1960s a change began to take place in the developing world as mass production initiatives were replaced by the production of goods and services in response to consumer tastes. Markets became increasingly diversified, so that manufacturers had to listen more closely to their potential customers, or risk losing business to their competitors. Advertising and marketing companies thrived, as they helped manufacturers "position" their products, gauge customer satisfaction, and solicit their suggestions for improvements and innovations. The result is that in today's consumer societies we are overwhelmed with choices.

Consumerism is not confined to the goods and services that we utilize. It also exercises a powerful influence on our attitudes and engagement with every institution in which we become involved: our choice of neighborhoods, schools, medical plans, recreational activities—and churches. In the days when communities were static and deeply rooted, churches consisted of congregations that were both engaged and conformist. For the majority of churchgoers, the church they attended represented the church tradition into which they had been born, rather than a church they had chosen to join. Pastors and priests could rely on the support of a dependable group of volunteers to run the programs for every age group and need.

In the past five decades, however, churchgoers have shifted from being conformers to being consumers. They attend a particular church as a matter of personal choice and can just as easily decide to leave and go elsewhere—or to drop out altogether. Such instability is further exacerbated by the mobility of our society. Cities continue to expand and suburbs mushroom, with people moving every few years in response to job relocations, their desire to find a bigger home, or the need to eventually move to a retirement community.

Consumerism continues to be a major challenge faced by churches, no matter what their theological orientation or ecclesial tradition, for it is deeply rooted and endemic in our society. Megachurches, which we will consider in greater depth in chapter 4, are in my view unfairly targeted as the main promoters of a consumerist approach to Christian ministry, when in reality the vast majority of churches, regardless of size, are similarly tainted.

From Religious Identity to Spiritual Exploration

Most sociologists in the 1960s predicted that the emergence of secular society would bring about the demise of religion. This supposition has proven to be half right as we have witnessed the demise of traditional religious institutions represented by what were termed the "mainline" churches. These churches, most of which trace their roots to the historic churches of Europe, are indeed suffering chronic numerical decline. But sociologists were mistaken in their biased assumption that religious interest would wane. Quite the opposite has occurred, with the majority of people still considering themselves as "spiritual." Significant numbers of churchgoers have simply changed their allegiance from the denomination in which they were nurtured as children to independent churches or churches of other traditions. They are looking for alternatives that offer an inspiring worship environment and that provide ministries that respond to their needs, or that demonstrate social awareness and community involvement.

Perhaps the most significant development has been among those who consider themselves "spiritual" but who do not identify with any institutional expression of Christianity. They may have moved to a more privatized faith, with some organizing themselves into home-based groups. These may flourish for a while, but will they have the resources to pass on their faith to the next generation? That remains an open question.

In our increasingly pluralistic society, to be "spiritual" does not necessarily signify a commitment to orthodox Christian beliefs. It is more likely to represent an eclectic spirituality, drawing not only from the various streams of Christian theology—Catholic, Orthodox, Episcopal, and Pentecostal—but including elements of other religious insights—Buddhism, Jewish mysticism, Hinduism, and Islam. Individuals mix their own spiritual potpourri. Such socially affirmed, religious eclecticism is also to be found among members of traditional congregations who have imbibed the spirit of the age.

Delayed Adulthood

Commitment to the morphing of the church takes on special urgency when we look to the "emerging adult" generation, which according to recent sociological research and telephone surveys is far less connected to and sympathetic toward the church and Christian beliefs.

Christian Smith quotes the research of Don Miller and James Heft, who describe young adulthood as a "mysterious black hole" in the life of the American church.[10] Smith also refers to Jeffrey Arnett's findings arising from his interviews with one hundred young adults, which revealed "how little relationship there is between the religious training they received throughout childhood and the religious beliefs they hold at the time they reached emerging adulthood." According to his statistical analysis "there was *no* relationship between exposure to religious training in childhood and *any* aspect of their religious beliefs as emerging adults."[11]

Whereas in previous decades the strength of the evangelical movement was among young people, these same people, having come to a personal faith in Christ, may not express their faith in terms of ongoing loyalty, either to their evangelical tradition or to the church that represents that ethos. They do not have a strong sense of allegiance to the "brand name" of the place where they make their spiritual home. For instance, a study by LifeWay Research that examined attendance rates at the annual meeting of the Southern Baptist Convention found that eighteen- to thirty-nine-year-olds make up a steadily decreasing proportion of the overall attendance totals at the meeting each year, ranging from almost 36 percent in 1985 to just over 13 percent in 2007.[12] Whether these numbers are simply a stark reminder of the need, as Trevin Wax observes, to "bridge the generation gap" so that young and old alike can learn from one another more readily, or whether they point to a larger trend of waning denominational loyalty among younger people, they certainly merit further consideration.[13]

The picture is filled in further by the presence of a countermovement to that of the emerging, missional churches. This countermovement represents a groundswell of local initiatives that explore new models and raise disturbing questions. The resurgence of a new conservatism adds another layer of complexity, as dispensationalism, fundamentalism, and Reformed streams become increasingly appealing to a segment of younger evangelicals. While these movements continue to grow, it is too soon to say to what extent they represent the evangelizing of de-churched and never-churched persons. At the present time, they appear mainly to be attracting younger Christians who are seeking a more coherent biblical and theological position, rather than one dictated by the surrounding culture. In the following chapter we will explore some of the characteristics that many of these initiatives share.

As the Builder generation dies off and the Boomer generation heads for retirement, the Church is facing a bleak future if it fails to make a greater impact among the under-35s. As we have seen in this chapter, the issue will not be adequately addressed merely by the development of new worship styles and programs to relate to the younger generations. Churches are increasingly out of touch because they have largely failed to recognize the deep and comprehensive nature of the transitions—what we have referred to here as "megatrends"—that are impacting every area of life in the Western world. It is often only in retrospect that the realization dawns that an irreversible transition has taken place. In the eighteenth and nineteenth centuries, the churches of Europe similarly failed to recognize the extent and impact on every aspect of society of the changes accompanying the Industrial Revolution. Church leaders did too little too late, with the result that the cities that birthed the new industrial age grew at a phenomenal rate, while the migrant populations became largely lost to the church. Churches today must take care not to repeat the mistakes of the past.

Summary

As we are now in the midst of the turmoil occasioned by the five transitions we have identified—from modernity to postmodernity; from the industrial to the information age; from Christendom to post-Christendom contexts; from production initiatives to consumer awareness; and from religious identity to spiritual exploration—we must learn the lesson of history: In the long term, churches will either morph or become moribund. But the process will be gradual and the picture confusing. As the Christendom mindset of traditional denominationalism fades with the passing of the Builder generation, the retiring Boomers will exert increasing influence in an endeavor to maintain their church tradition, characterized by individualism and consumerism. But even though they represent a numerically large and affluent generation, they are likely, with increased life expectancy and the resulting escalation in retirement costs, to become progressively less generous in their financial support of the churches.

Both individually and collectively, the five megatrends we have identified in this chapter represent a formidable challenge to churches. They point to a need for congregations to locate resources—both within themselves and from outside agencies with expertise in relating the gospel to specific segments of the cultural mosaic—that can lend insight and experience to their journey along the road that lies ahead. Churches must seek out mission partners committed to assisting Christians in their witness from the margins of society within religious and culturally pluralistic contexts.

2

post-christendom churches

In response to the current disquiet concerning the state of the churches in the Western world, three initiatives have gained widespread attention. These are the missional church movement, the emerging church phenomenon, and, in the UK context, Fresh Expressions (which will be discussed in detail in the following chapter), an umbrella term promoted by traditional denominations to cover a wide range of initiatives.

The Missional Church

The most coherent of the above developments, the missional church arose out of the Gospel and Our Culture Network, inspired by a small group of scholars who developed the thinking of Lesslie Newbigin, which originally arose out of his concern for the churches in Europe. On his return from India, where he had served as a bishop in the Church of South India, Newbigin recognized that the United Kingdom in particular, and Europe in general, posed a missional challenge as great as anywhere in the world. In many respects it posed a tougher challenge in that the church had become widely discredited in the popular mind and the Christian message had lost potency, because there was so little evidence of its impact in the lives of those who professed the Christian faith.

The coherence of the missional church movement was further strengthened by a series of seven books published by Eerdmans that provided an authoritative source for academics and church leaders who were concerned with the numerical decline and diminishing influence of Christian churches throughout North America.[1] The first of these appeared in 1996 and began by acknowledging indebtedness to Lesslie Newbigin's writing in developing a domestic missiology for North America. Two years later, the urgency of the situation was spelled out in the following terms:

> The crises are certainly many and complex: diminishing numbers, clergy burnout, the loss of youth, the end of denominational loyalty, biblical illiteracy, divisions in the ranks, the electronic church and its various corruptions, the irrelevance of traditional forms of worship, the loss of genuine spirituality, and widespread confusion about both the purpose and the message of Jesus Christ.[2]

In the decade that has passed since that assessment, there is no evidence of the situation having improved; rather, it has worsened. As the de-churched generation is joined by the growing ranks of the never-churched, the missional challenge becomes increasingly urgent. Alan Roxburgh, a Canadian Baptist who travels extensively throughout North America, the United Kingdom, and Australia consulting with a wide range of denominations and independent groups, issues the following challenge to the churches:

> If the West is once again a mission field within which the central narratives of the gospel have been lost or profoundly compromised by other values, then the focus of this *mission* must be upon placing the God who has encountered us in Jesus Christ back in the center of our communities of faith that shape and give meaning to our

lives. This may seem an obvious part of being a Christian, but it is not happening in our American churches today.[3]

The contribution of the missional church movement lies in the challenge it issues to the churches of North America that they become authentically missional, as well as in the theological undergirding that it has provided. It has coined the term "missional" to emphasize the fact that the church should not think of mission as an activity relating exclusively, or even principally, to distant parts of the world. Mission begins at the threshold of the church. It relates to the very identity of the church, not to a prescribed activity. By its very nature, the church is both the product and the vehicle of God's mission in the world. As such, it becomes the principal agent of the reign of God, providing "salt" and "light" in society.

Whereas the missional church movement is strong on theory, it struggles to transfer its insights into the life of local churches. Many church leaders have adopted missional church language without evidencing significant change in their modus operandi. The gap between academia and local church is a wide one to bridge. It is one thing to adopt the language of the missional church, but what are the evidences of a church that is authentically missional in its ethos and engagement? Alan Hirsch identifies the following six elements of "Apostolic Genius," a characteristic "that imbues phenomenal Jesus movements in history," especially in the early church, but that is lacking within many churches today:[4]

1. *Jesus Is Lord*: At the center and circumference of every Jesus movement there exists a very simple confession . . . namely, that of the claim of one God over every aspect of every life, and the response of his people to that claim (Deut. 6:4–6ff.).
2. *Disciple-Making*: Essentially this involves the irreplaceable, and lifelong, task of becoming like Jesus by embodying his message. . . . Disciple-making is an irreplaceable core task of the church and needs to be structured into every church's basic formula.
3. *Missional-Incarnational Impulse*: [This is] the dynamic outward thrust and the related deepening impulse which together

seed and embed the gospel into different cultures and people groups.

4. *Apostolic Environment*: [This is] the fertile environment that [apostolic influence] creates in initiating and maintaining the phenomenal movements of God. This will relate to the type of leadership and ministry required to sustain metabolic growth and impact.

5. *Organic Systems*: [This is] the idea of appropriate structures for metabolic growth. Phenomenal Jesus movements grow precisely because they do not have centralized institutions to block growth through control. . . . Jesus movements have the feel of a movement, have structure as a network, and spread like viruses.

6. Communitas *Not Community*: The most vigorous forms of community are those that come together in the context of a shared ordeal or those that define themselves as a group with a mission that lies beyond themselves—thus initiating a risky journey.[5]

In my view the missional church movement's theological grounding and cultural insights need to be linked with the emerging church's missional engagement in specific contexts for their mutual enrichment. Theory and praxis need to go hand-in-hand.

The Emerging Church

The emerging church phenomenon's strength lies at the grassroots level at which it operates. Its theory arises from its praxis—and is consequently more diverse and less coherent. It embraces a wide spectrum of practices and theological antecedents, being a ground level–up, spontaneous phenomenon and not a top-down, orchestrated movement. It represents a wide range of local initiatives and strategic alliances, as opposed to top-down organizational entities, each with its "brand label" and strategies. It is difficult to categorize, in that it does not represent a particular doctrinal stance. It is not a confessional movement identified by a "statement of faith" to which all are expected to subscribe. Neither is it confined to one ecclesial tradition.

Alan Hirsch draws a helpful distinction between the emerging and missional streams: "I tend to think of emerging church as a renewal movement rather than a purely missional one. In other words, mission is not the organizing principle but rather worship and theology in a postmodern setting. This is good and well, but it is not necessarily a truly missionary activity."[6] In order to address his concern I believe that we need to see an intermingling of the two streams so that each can complement and enrich the other.

Emerging churches are to be found within inherited denominations, in addition to being represented by new networks and an array of independent initiatives. John Drane comments, "While deeply embedded in a particular faith tradition, many are using the term as creative license to reignite their congregations. It becomes an umbrella term under which a wide array of thoughts, theologies, ideologies, and intentions come together."[7] Rather than being a single movement it consists of a number of streams that diverge and converge and then create new tributaries. True to its label, it continues to be an "emerging" movement that cannot be encapsulated in precise definitions. The following chapters, each devoted to a principal stream, will evidence this overlap.

As a wide variety of groups become conversant with emergent issues, largely as a result of Web-based connectivity that reaches beyond denominational structures and traditions, the emergent stream is becoming increasingly ecumenical. Its Web-based structure allows it to challenge hierarchies that attempt to monopolize channels of communication. The dramatically increasing number of Web sites, chat rooms, blogs, and wikis has helped facilitate the creation of its own ethos.

Precisely because the emerging church is a ground-level phenomenon, it is impossible to track comprehensively or quantify precisely. Studies of the early church present a similar challenge. Each "household"-based church was reproducible. Consequently the early church was structured for exponential growth. A recent study of secular businesses has drawn attention to the dynamic of leaderless organizations.[8] The authors, Ori Brafman and Rod Beckstrom, draw an important distinction between the spider and the starfish. A spider can be destroyed by stepping on its head. The starfish, however, presents a more difficult challenge. If you cut off the leg of a starfish, it grows another, and the severed leg develops into a new starfish. The early churches resembled starfish rather than spiders. The church father Tertullian made a similar observation when he commented that "the blood of the martyrs is the seed of the church."

Some critics of the emerging church phenomenon have based their negative judgment on statements made by one or more of its leading exponents or on opinions that were formed after attending a conference that provided a platform for high-profile speakers. They have concluded both that the emerging church consists largely of a generation of younger leaders who are angry with institutional Christianity and that their hostility has blinded them to the direction in which they are heading on the rebound and where it will eventually lead them. One senior conservative church leader has even castigated it as "an end-time deception."

Admittedly, some individuals and groups are clearer on what they are *against* than on what they are *for*. As an emerging phenomenon, elements are heading in different directions. Any critique must take into account their wide-ranging theological and ecclesial diversity. They combine liturgical and non-liturgical, liberal and conservative, charismatic and contemplative approaches, as well as evangelistic and social engagement, personal piety, and corporate disciplines.

It is my personal observation that many of the emerging church leaders who are most strident in their criticism represent those who are reacting against the legalistic, fundamentalist contexts in which they themselves were reared, while others are seeking more honest answers, and a more comprehensive social agenda, than that offered by either the charismatic or holiness traditions of their past. The confusing diversity of emerging churches represents both a reaction to the evangelical tendency to draw boundaries to determine who is in and who is out and a postmodern celebration of ambiguity and diversity.

Some of the attempts at mission engagement made by emerging church leaders may have been clumsy or even misguided, but at least they represent sincere efforts to address the chronic and increasingly urgent challenges facing churches of all traditions in the West. Some expressions of emergence will be transient, and some diversionary. Hopefully, among the latter, some will self-correct as they learn from their misdirection and failures, while others may well head off into obscurity or become subverted by yesterday's outmoded liberal assumptions. In the course of the long history of mission, many such mistakes have been made, and if we do not know that history, we have set ourselves up to repeat it.

Sara Savage and Eolene Boyd-MacMillan, research associates with the Psychology and Religion Research Group at the University of Cambridge, caution that "fresh expressions" of emerging churches are not immune from the "routinization of charisma," to quote Max Weber's famous phrase.

> Even with the Body of Christ, the life-giving *charism* has to be embodied in a routine—in some form of human organization. Yet, life-giving visions do not fit easily into neat boxes. So, the very process that gives the vision continuing life also begins to kill it. When the maintenance of the institution (which protects the *charism*) becomes the institution's primary purpose, the death of the *charism* is on the horizon. Only a spiritual revival or reform will re-ignite the gift. In our era, fresh expressions of church and the re-traditioning of familiar forms of church march alongside many initiatives to re-ignite the gift.[9]

Leaders of emerging churches need to be especially aware of the process of routinization throughout the group. "Although not leaderless, the emerging church is more of a 'grass roots', 'bottom-up' endeavour. However, Weber's concept of the 'routinization of *charisma*' warns us that whatever the structure of our group, over time there is a natural slide towards conforming to the dominant behaviour and opinions of the group."[10]

As we have noted, emerging churches defy classification. Because of the dynamic nature of the phenomenon, they create streams that merge and divide, and, because of a disdain of labels and of being containerized, they are vulnerable to subversion by any and all who lay claim to the label without expressing the reality. Emerging churches represent a spirit of wide-ranging intellectual curiosity, producing an eclectic spirituality that draws from a variety of church traditions in regard to its forms of worship and expressions of mission. Doug Pagitt of Solomon's Porch expresses this eclecticism in describing his church as "kinda like a liturgical church, and . . . kinda like a Mennonite church, and . . . kinda like a Bible church, etc. . . . because they incorporate valuable elements from all of those traditions."[11]

In contrast to the mainstream of North American evangelicalism in which the various "tribes" define and defend themselves in terms of their boundaries, emerging churches are more concerned with putting down roots in a wide range of traditions. They believe this is what is entailed in becoming truly catholic. Many emerging congregations are made up of members from a variety of traditions. They join together as a congregation with the approval of their parent denominations. For instance, in Chicago the Church of Jesus Christ, Reconciler, led by Tripp Hudkins, combines Anglican, American Baptist, and Evangelical Covenant, while in Sheffield, England, St. Thomas' Crookes Philadelphia Center joins Anglican, Baptist, and the independent King's Church.

Kester Brewin draws an important distinction between "emerging" and "Emergent": "The *emerging church* is a label that is being stuck on anything outside the 'norms' of the church as most people know it; whereas the *Emergent Church* is specifically about the principles of the science of emergence to church growth."[12] Scot McKnight makes a different distinction:

> Emerging is the wider, informal, global, ecclesial (church-centered) focus of the movement, while Emergent is an official organization in the U.S. and the U.K. Emergent Village, the organization, is directed by Tony Jones, a Ph.D. student at Princeton Theological Seminary and a world traveler on behalf of all things both Emergent and emerging.[13]

In order to rescue the term "emerging church" from being misunderstood as simply a reactive or trendy expression of church, I have blended the terms "emerging" and "missional" in this book.[14] To the extent that emerging churches fail to follow the lead of the early churches by engaging in the mission that reproduces faith communities, they will be short-lived and leave little in the way of a legacy to celebrate.

Shared Convictions

In our consideration of the morphing of the church, we will embrace the wider category of "emerging." Since, however, we are concerned primarily with the missional engagement of the church, we will critique both the emerging and the missional stream in terms of their recognition of the church's fundamental nature as a body that does not live for itself, but serves as Christ's appointed agent in the worldwide mission of God. As the missional church and a significant segment of the emerging church together represent a concern to redefine the church in post-Christendom, missional terms, they should not be regarded as conflicting entities, but rather as complementary and converging approaches; the former represents a more deductive approach, while the latter is more inductive. The two streams need to meet each other rather than pass like strangers in the night.

Each has attracted a following and has given rise to a body of literature and sponsored conferences on a regular basis. There has been an increasing tendency for churches to identify themselves as either missional or emerging. But it is easier to attach a label than it is to demonstrate the essential characteristics of either stream. Denominational executives and local church pastors tend to look for the next program that will provide momentum for the ongoing life of the church. Over the past five decades of church decline, we have witnessed a succession of programs, each offering hope to the church. They have all come and gone without being able to deliver on their promises, unable to reverse the downward numerical trends.

The last thing that exponents of missional and emerging churches want is for their vision and insights to become yet another add-on program to a church that remains fundamentally unchanged. They both call for a radical re-envisioning of the church in response to the deep-level, comprehensive, cultural transitions described in the previous chapter. We must therefore draw from the insights of both the missional and emerging streams to identify the insights they hold in common, as well as the distinctive contributions made by each. They have the potential not only to complement but also to challenge each other.

Perhaps the time has come to drop the labels, as each has accu-
mulated baggage and led to a new "tribalism." Their diversity and
loose networks mean that they lack cohesion. I agree with Kester
Brewin's recent blog comment expressing his hunch that

> some of the key players are less and less willing to work with that
> particular language [i.e., of labels, such as "emerging"]. I think that,
> whereas a few years ago people were excited by the prospect, people
> are getting used to/bored/fed up with "emerging church" as a concept,
> and will thus leave it behind.
>
> Not that I think that that means "game over" for all that people
> like Emergent stand for—far from it actually—but I think people
> may increasingly assimilate those ideas into their practice without
> taking the name. (I think for some time this has been foreseen in
> the collapse in usefulness of the term "emerging church," which is
> so tired as a phrase it has begun to mean nothing.)
>
> I think people have become tired of a whole lot of talking, and
> want to see things actually happen . . . and when stuff actually hap-
> pens, it tends to be quieter and create less internet hum than the
> talking about it.[15]

The emerging church phenomenon must not degenerate into
disputations over theological positions. Critics applying theological
litmus tests are drawing battle lines, with an increasing number of
negative responses to the emerging church.[16] Its basic goal must
be commitment to mission in post-Christendom contexts, a commitment that will help reforge the link between ecclesiology and
missiology.

Common Characteristics

The diversity of the missional expressions of church that we will be
covering in the following chapters means that a list of characteristics,
such as those I consulted in preparing this section, can be expanded
indefinitely, with the result that any given church will only exhibit a
few of the features described. Consequently, the following are offered
as representing those most commonly identified by churches that

are in the process of becoming both missional and emerging. For a more comprehensive list of distinctive features, see the appendix at the back of this book.

Dependence on God Permeates the Life of the Faith Community

There is a growing recognition that human strategies and know-how are totally inadequate as means to bringing individuals to a vital faith and to birthing and growing vibrant churches. The "new birth" of which Jesus spoke is a birth from above, with only God able to bring about the miracle of regeneration, through the indwelling of the Holy Spirit. Human ingenuity and effort may be able to gather a crowd, but only the miracles of reconciliation and regeneration can bring into being a local expression of the body of Christ. It is important to grasp this point, especially when working among apathetic and spiritually resistant populations, in which many have abandoned the church precisely because they did not perceive it to be spiritual enough.

When theological positions are based on rationalistic presuppositions, whether of the liberal or fundamentalist varieties, there tends to be more eloquent speaking and writing about prayer than actual practice of prayer. In spiritualities that focus on engagement with God in worship and intercession, there is more evidence of the classic, spiritual disciplines being observed and developed. We see this in Roman Catholic, Orthodox, holiness, Pentecostal, and charismatic churches. Barry Taylor suggests that "resources for dealing with the nonrational, the plural, and the mysterious are in short supply in evangelicalism, given its rationalizing tendencies."[17] In part, the emerging church phenomenon represents a reaction to such rationalism, as individuals and communities seek deeper levels of personal encounter with God and a corporate response to his breaking them down for the sake of restoration, his empowering, and his leading.

Heartbeat of the Church Is to Communicate the Gospel

The church obeys the Great Commission to make disciples among all peoples (Matt. 28:19) as a privilege and not simply an obligation.

The proclamation of the gospel is the constant mission of the church. It is its heartbeat, and not simply an occasional and uncomfortable hiccup in its life. The church shares the apostle Paul's conviction and passion to declare the good news and has an unshakeable confidence in the power of the gospel to bring about a radical and comprehensive transformation in the lives of individuals and the communities to which they belong (Rom. 1:16–17). But in order to proclaim a transforming message, the faith community must demonstrate the impact of that message on its corporate life, as it interfaces with people in every area of daily life. It witnesses as much by its being and doing as by what it says. Demonstration must go hand-in-hand with proclamation.

Faith Communities Are Birthed among the Never-Churched and the De-Churched

From a missional perspective, the missional and emergent streams will only gain significance as they reach out to the de-churched and never-churched segments of the population, rather than providing the latest attraction for bored, frustrated, or angry current church-goers. They also need to be strongly in evidence in urban contexts, recognizing that our culture is driven by urban values and images, with suburbia increasingly becoming culturally marginalized. Within urban contexts, their appeal needs to extend beyond the artsy elites to fully embrace the multicultural nature of their social setting. As one black urban church leader expressed, "Urban means more than white guys with goatees!"

The call to mission and emergence entails embarking on a process of self-analysis that may prove profoundly unsettling. George Hunsberger cautions,

> We are warned against conceiving the "gospel and culture" encounter as one that is merely a matter of audience analysis, as though it has only to do with sizing up the thoughts, feelings and values of the target population to make our communication of the gospel sharper. Nor is it adequate to conceive of the encounter as merely our effort to bring about changes in the personal and collective ethical choices of the

society so that they more closely approximate the ideals we see to be those of the gospel. . . . These responses represent the persistence of an 'us to them' mission mentality too easily operating out of a conquering spirit or an urge to control, vestiges of former Christendom that no longer lives anywhere but in the impulses of our minds.[18]

Communities Demonstrate the Transforming Power of the Gospel

The impact of the witness of the early church was not primarily in the signs and wonders that were in evidence in its ministries of healing and deliverance; it also arose from its demonstration of Christ-inspired, self-sacrificing love. When members behave badly toward one another the church's witness inevitably is compromised. Precisely because the gospel is a message of profound reconciliation between sinful humankind and a holy God, its effectiveness needs to be demonstrated by communities that are learning how to practice reconciliation. A divided church is a denial of its essential nature. Witness consists of the corporate testimony of the church that is struggling to live out the demands of the gospel in the power of the Spirit. Community is only possible when members submit to mutual accountability.

Evidence of personal and relational transformation within its corporate life is a necessary prerequisite for the church, in order for it to have a significant positive impact on society. Before it can hope to attract people into its community, it must genuinely and impartially engage in society. This is especially important where churches are regarded with suspicion by people who believe that they have an ulterior motive and that their social engagement is simply a manipulative recruitment ploy.

Worship Provides the Inspiration for Mission

The worship of missional and emerging churches is God-focused, rather than seeking to enhance the celebrity status of the preacher or worship leaders—it is "the central act by which the community celebrates with joy and thanksgiving both God's presence and God's promised future."[19] Under Christendom, a wedge was driven between the *life* of the church and the *mission* of the church. The latter was all too frequently departmentalized, marginalized, and distanced from the church. Worship that fails to renew the church's commitment to mission is little more than spiritual self-indulgence. We will look at this issue in greater detail in the final chapter.

Emerging missional churches express their cultural engagement by the inclusion of the entire worshiping community as creative participants, which makes for varied and lively worship. Worship leaders introduce the best of contemporary worship songs and creative elements, yet the main content of their worship gatherings is home produced. They write their own songs and develop elements that involve the active participation of the congregation, in hopes of heightening the impact of the message and leading to a new depth of understanding. The act of worship embraces the entire congregation, regardless of age or level of spiritual maturity or religious enculturation. It is not elitist, confined to the platform performance of the professionals or even of talented amateurs. It is liturgy that is accessible because it is *of* the people, even though it may draw from centuries of Christian tradition. It also provides opportunity *for* the people—every person, in fact—to tell their story and contribute from their insights, experience, gifting, and calling. And because it is within the family, a light-hearted playfulness prevails. Members recognize that a critical spirit inhibits, and sometimes even paralyzes, participation, often causing hurt and damage to the individuals toward whom it is directed.

Corporate Life of Worship, Fellowship, and Witness Is Appropriate to the Cultural Context

A crucial distinction needs to be made at the outset between naive contextualization and critical contextualization. While the church needs to be birthed within its cultural context, it does not simply mirror its values. "The church understands itself as different from the world because of its participation in the life, death, and resurrection of its Lord."[20]

Under the influence of modernity, attempts were made to franchise successful models of church without due regard either for the distinctive histories and internal dynamics of the church or for its specific ministry contexts. Recognizing that each church is a manifestation of the body of Christ, birthed and nurtured in its own ministry environment, churches cannot be franchised after the model of McDonald's or Colonel Sanders' Kentucky Fried Chicken outlets. Rather than attempting to import a model from elsewhere, every local church must discern God's calling in regard to his purposes and the specifics of their situation, as well as to each individual's own unique history, gifts, and passion.

Practice of Hospitality Means that All Who Come Are Welcomed

The practice of hospitality by a local church cannot be restricted to those within the Christian fellowship that members have selected as their friends; neither can it be confined to the church at large, as though it were a private, self-selecting, self-serving club advertising for new members. In order for "loving our neighbor" to become the fulfillment of the law, we must recognize, according to Professor Cranfield, that it "involves not just loving someone other than oneself, but loving *each* person whom God presents to one as one's neighbour by the circumstance of his being someone whom one *is in a position* to affect for good or ill. The 'neighbour' in the New Testament sense is not someone arbitrarily chosen by us: he is given to us by God."[21] As Paul makes clear in his letter to the church in Rome, love is an unpaid debt (Rom. 13:8–10). No matter how much we endeavor to discharge it we will always owe it, because the love of Christ knows no limits.

Hospitality entails not only a seat in the church, but a place at the table. The missional church is one that welcomes all comers, regardless of their lifestyle and beliefs, but always with a view to their radical transformation. Discipleship entails a change of direction in order to follow Christ, which only becomes possible through the reconciling love of Christ and the indwelling of his Spirit in the life of the believer. Furthermore, all Christians equally are involved in that transformation process, from those just embarking on their faith journey to those who have walked together in company with

Christ for many years. Christian discipleship entails a lifelong commitment to learning and growing.

The Way of Jesus Is Interpreted within a Specific Place and Time

All the members are earnestly seeking to become authentic followers of Christ. This entails, in the first place, exploring the significance of the gospel of the kingdom as it is elaborated in the account of the ministry and teaching of Jesus. Next comes the challenge of transposing that teaching to the issues encountered today by believers in their diverse life situations. By focusing attention on the gospel in the Gospels, emergent preachers and teachers capture the centrality of the gospel message, which is not primarily about the individual and his or her salvation, but about the coming of Jesus to establish the reign of God on earth, and the outpouring of the Holy Spirit to provide the channel for that message to be appropriated and lived out, at least in provisional form.

The gospel story also makes clear that the message of the cross of Jesus and the significance of his resurrection and ascension make sense only if we are first made aware of the person, message, and ministry of Jesus, as recorded in the Gospels. These accounts do not *begin with* the cross but all *lead to* the cross. The climactic significance of the events of the final weeks of Jesus' life spent journeying to Jerusalem, and his last week teaching in the Temple, are emphasized by the disproportionate amount of space they occupy in the narrative. In sharing the gospel with today's generations that are increasingly ignorant of the story of Jesus, we must likewise present a message that leads to the cross, but that does not begin there.

Evangelization is not an end in itself, but rather an invitation to a life of discipleship. Unfortunately, discipleship has become an elitist concept, referring to those who are "really serious" about their faith commitment. Much evangelization has focused on the decision itself to the neglect of the change of allegiance that such a decision entails. Addressing this disconnect entails first the need to address, as a matter of urgency, the challenge of undiscipled church members. They will need to be engaged with great patience, as well as persistence, in that little was expected of them under the norms of Christendom. Furthermore, missional church leaders cannot restrict their teaching to issues of personal morality and the development of the internal life of the church. They must be prepared to walk alongside their members and to acquaint themselves with the complex issues that they face, both in the workplace and within the broader culture.

Everyone Is Clustered within Face-to-Face, Interactive Communities

The cluster provides mutual support, encourages accountability, develops ministry and mission potential, and facilitates a climate for leadership development.[22] It provides a corporate structure by which the church is able to continue to function in dispersion. Each cluster develops its own life that represents its context and calling. It ensures that the church doesn't live for itself, within its own "bubble," but that it is identified with both its surrounding neighborhood and other locations where clusters of believers begin to form.

In addition to neighborhood clusters, which form around a shared geographic location, other types of clusters may be formed around shared affinities and interests, including sports, lifestyle, hobbies, and special needs, such as being physically or mentally challenged. In the absence of this kind of decentralized clustering, individual Christians are left to bear their witness, often in isolation. Their witness becomes more powerful expressed as the choral statement of a group of believers, which, in its corporate life, demonstrates the values and spiritual resources of the reign of Christ. Clustering makes the church accessible because each expression is localized and contextually appropriate.

A decentralized, nodular network enables the church to remain flexible and responsive to changing local circumstances. Clustering represents a commitment to connecting, rather than protecting, corralled believers. There is an essential missional dimension to each cluster, expressed in a determination to reach out to their wider network of relationships and beyond. Each cluster is eager to welcome the stranger. Cluster members are uninhibited in their eagerness to celebrate the presence of God in their midst, as they mingle with the wider community. Incarnational witness entails a genuine sense of belonging and identity before it can realize its vision for societal transformation. In so doing, it is expressing the inclusion of Jesus, as he sat at the table with the social outcasts of his day in a nonjudgmental way.

Commitment to community, with mutual accountability, constitutes a great challenge to churchgoers who have bought into an individualistic, consumer culture mentality. This has bred a casual, or contractual, relationship to the church, whereby the individual dictates his or her own terms of membership. But the church, understood as the body of Christ—one of the dominant biblical images—does not consist of a clientele, such as regular movie theater or restaurant goers. Those individuals decide from day to day on the frequency of their attendance and keep their options open to go elsewhere, should they so choose. In contrast, the body of Christ is made up of members who constitute the limbs and organs of the body. They cannot come and go at will, and their absence causes both loss of bodily functions and pain to the other members (1 Cor. 12:14–26).

The Gospel Relates to the Whole of Life

Modernity drives a wedge between the realms of the sacred and the secular, and in so doing, marginalizes the sacred. It deliberately excludes the sacred from the centers of power and influence in society. In consequence, religion becomes both individualized and privatized, to the extent that Christians find themselves living in two largely unrelated worlds.

The emerging missional church seeks to break down that sacred/secular divide, pointing to its devastating social consequences. In its place, it advocates a holistic spirituality, embracing every aspect of life. It is committed not just to social service, but also to issues of justice, which often lie behind the social ills that it seeks to ameliorate. It represents a life-embracing spirituality, rather than one that seeks separation from the world. The church has a vital public witness that is not limited to the this-world emphasis of the Social Gospel advocates associated with the liberal traditions of the past, but that seeks to celebrate and actualize the presence of the ascended Lord in every area of life.

The younger emerging church leaders regard the social activism of previous generations as tainted by the modernistic sacred/secular divide of the past. They recognize that human effort and political maneuvering will not bring about the reign of Christ. We cannot build the kingdom; rather, in the teaching of Jesus, the coming of the kingdom is the prerogative of God, and comes as gift and surprise. Consequently, in their social engagement, emerging church leaders are also passionate about Jesus. Yet, this witness is not with a triumphal, crusading spirit, but with humility, recognizing that God always gets there before we do, for the kingdom is more extensive than the church. All too often the church has tragically failed in this regard, as a result of either lack of vision for the expansiveness of God's reign or reluctance to commit to following that larger vision.

The younger leaders of the emerging church are engaged in popular culture, believing that there are clear evidences of God's prevenient grace in the spiritual aspirations that permeate, for example, popular songs and magazine articles.[23] They believe that the stance of the church is not to confront popular culture, but to engage it from within. Every culture is made up of a complex mix of elements that the gospel affirms, while at the same time exposing demeaning and destructive values that run contrary to the kingdom message of Jesus. This is as true of the culture of modernity as of postmodernity—of "high" culture as of "popular" culture.

Entire Body Is Engaged in the Church's Ministry and Mission

The prevalence of the consumer mentality among church members poses one of the biggest challenges to churches desiring to transition into becoming missional. During the decade of the seventies, there was a spate of books and seminars emphasizing the ministry of the whole people of God through the recognition and activation of gift-based ministries. One of the most influential books of the period was that of C. Peter Wagner, *Your Spiritual Gifts Can Help Your Church Grow* (Regal Press, 1979). Despite widespread interest in the issue of gift-based ministry, it soon became evident that simply preaching sermons and leading seminars did not automatically result in the burgeoning of every-member ministries, for such diverse ministries do not emerge in highly controlled environments.

Insecure leaders are easily threatened by people who are more gifted than they are or who are gifted in different areas. Consequently, they tend to surround themselves with individuals who aspire to be like them, or with people of lesser ability. Spiritual gifts do not primarily emerge by means of individuals completing gift identification questionnaires, but in the context of community participation. In other words, ministry flows from relationships. And relationships flourish when leaders give permission, provide encouragement, and serve as mentors. As people explore and develop their gifts, they need opportunities and advocates.

Gradually, controlling and delegating modes of leadership are giving way to more collaborative and empowering styles. This change is partly as a consequence of the advent of the information age, coupled with a move from hierarchies and controls to networking and empowerment. We are experiencing today what Harlan Cleveland has described as the twilight of the hierarchies: "The shift is now more than obvious: from top-down vertical relationships towards horizontal, consensual, collaborative modes of getting people together to make something different happen."[24]

Furthermore, whereas gifts were once described almost exclusively in terms of the internal agendas and programs of the local church, and church leaders, for the most part, did not explore their significance for the manifold ministries of the people of God in the world, a significant shift in emphasis is taking place in the missional and emergent streams: from ministry *within* the people of God to ministry *by* the people of God in the furtherance of its God-given mission. This shift necessarily entails a re-examination of the significance of the gifts of the Holy Spirit in relation to life lived in the workplace and elsewhere.

The Bible Is a Guide for Life's Journey

The Scriptures are not primarily a repository of facts and information that provide a test of a person's orthodoxy. Neither are they a collection of proof texts that one can edit in order to extract those portions that support preconceptions while, at the same time, ignoring the challenges they may pose to our priorities. Tom Sine comments that emerging church leaders display "little interest in the propositional, dogmatic approach to theology."[25] Rather, the whole of Scripture presents a coherent story. It is a narrative of the unfolding revelation of God's purposes and provisions for humankind. It provides a normative account—the Big Story, to which our little stories can be linked and transformed in the process.

Some have claimed that the postmodern approach rejects any and every metanarrative. But there is abundant evidence that many are simply searching for a metanarrative that brings a sense of meaning and significance to their lives. Suspicions associated with metanarratives arise from the ways in which they can be misused to disempower others in order to gain control. While a metanarrative is to be explored and *pro*posed, it can never be *im*posed on another person; browbeating a person into submission against his or her will is no substitute for genuine engagement.

Leadership Is Identified and Encouraged throughout the Body

Under the constraints of modernity, leadership tended to be an elitist concept, exercised through hierarchy and control. For churches to be effectively missional in a postmodern information age, leadership has to be devolved and expressed by different individuals according to the situational demands. Leadership consists of connecting people to one another. Missional churches encourage creative freedom and initiative taking, while at the same time providing the possibility of failing with dignity.[26] But freedom also requires accountability as a safeguard and to ensure a learning environment in which leaders mature through wise mentoring.

A learning system is one in which everyone is made aware of what is going on around them. It recognizes that no individual can know all that needs to be known, given the complexities of the world in which we live. It is a system that draws on the collective wisdom of the entire body. It constantly asks, "What do we need to know?"

and "Who is most likely to know?" The role of the overall leader is to serve as a catalyst in this process by identifying issues, making connections, and articulating and reiterating the vision so that the church has a sense of common mission that is linked to a multiplicity of callings, giftings, and tasks.

Every Church Recognizes Itself As an Incomplete Expression of the Reign of God

Every community of believers consists of individuals who are forgiven sinners at various stages in their lifelong walk of faith, and not perfected saints. For this reason, every church is an *emerging* church, precisely because it has not yet arrived; a *pilgrim* church that has not yet reached its destination; a *becoming* church that has not yet attained its fulfillment, which will only occur when the bridegroom comes for his bride (Rev. 19:7). As Kester Brewin emphasizes, the emerging church represents an open as opposed to a closed system. It is open to change from within, resisting the increasing pressure to provide a protective, insular environment.[27]

Summary

As both the missional and the emerging streams have developed their visions of churches engaging their particular cultural contexts within the larger post-Christendom context, their broad agreement on a number of fundamentals is apparent. They agree, for example, that "church" must be understood as referring to a people rather than to a place. A "congregation" represents not just a weekly gathering that people are a part of, but a community in which each person actively belongs, receives support, and is encouraged to make their own distinctive contribution. It consists not of passive consumers, but of creative participants. It is structured not just for attracting a congregation, but also for sending and dispersing people on a mission. It is comprised of an extensive network of clusters of believers providing mutual support, as well as engaging the broader networks of relationships of which they are a part.

The church is not primarily a place of refuge, but a community of people on pilgrimage.

In the following chapters we will provide numerous illustrations to serve as examples of the ways in which the characteristics identified and described in this chapter are being expressed in a variety of emerging churches committed to mission in their context.

interlude

identifying the streams

The following survey of the streams of emerging missional churches seeks to represent the dominant characteristic of each. The chapter to which each is assigned does not necessarily indicate the complete separation of one stream from another. For instance, a church that describes itself as an Alt.Worship (alternative worship) congregation may also have a strong commitment to mission, while an emerging church might be more self-preoccupied than missionally engaged.

A precursor to the emerging church consisted of house churches, in which small groups met to explore alternative ways of being church. A variety of networks and independent experiments gathered momentum in the decades of the eighties and nineties on both sides of the Atlantic. The house church influence continues today, in what has become known as "simple church." Sometimes these house groups separated in protest, declaring their complete independence from institutional Christianity. At other times, they represented an alternative, experimental structure in continuing relationship with a parent church. In Britain some of the early house church networks were represented by Pioneer,[1] often referred to as New

Church, founded by Gerald Coates; Ichthus,[2] a network of fifteen churches in the London area led by Roger Forster; and Revelation, led by Roger Ellis alongside his team.[3]

Attempts at Classification

A number of commentators have provided their own classification of the various streams that come under the category of "emerging" or "emergent." Scot McKnight, professor of religious studies at North Park University in Chicago,[4] identifies the following five streams:[5]

1. *Prophetic (or at least provocative)*: Believing that the church needs to change, the language within this stream often borrows from Old Testament rhetoric. Brian McLaren in the United States and Peter Rollins in Ireland are representative of this stream. They emphasize that the church needs to move from orthodoxy to orthopraxy.
2. *Postmodern*: "Postmodernity cannot be reduced to the denial of truth. Instead, it is the collapse of inherited metanarratives (overarching explanations of life) like those of science or Marxism. Why have they collapsed? Because of the impossibility of getting outside their assumptions" and, I would add, their failure to deliver on their promises.[6] "Emerging upholds faith seeking understanding, and trust preceding the apprehension or comprehension of gospel truths." Doug Pagitt of Solomon's Porch in Minneapolis says that some "will minister *to* postmoderns, others *with* postmoderns, and still others *as* postmoderns"; most fit the first two categories.[7]
3. *Praxis-oriented*: *Praxis* is the way in which faith is lived out and includes: worship that expresses the fact that God cares about sacred space and ritual; orthopraxy, which acknowledges that "experience does not prove that those who *believe* the right things *live* the right way"; and a missional approach, as seen in the lives of those who practice the way of Jesus

"by participating, with God, in the redemptive work of God in this world" (2 Cor. 5:18). "The church is the community through which God works and in which God manifests the credibility of the gospel. . . . The Spirit groans, the creation groans, and we groan for the redemption of God (see Rom. 8:18–27)."[8]

4. *Post-evangelical*: "It is post-evangelical in the way that neo-evangelicalism (in the 1950s) was post-fundamentalist." It is post-foundationalist. It is "suspicious of systematic theology. . . . God didn't reveal a systematic theology but a storied narrative, and no language is capable of capturing the Absolute Truth who alone is God." No systematic theology can be final. Furthermore, it is "skeptical about the 'in versus out' mentality of much of evangelicalism," emphasizing that there is "a wideness in God's mercy" and pointing to Jesus' saying: "whoever is not against us is for us" (Mark 9:40). Spencer Burke represents the extreme of this position in *A Heretic's Guide to Eternity* (Jossey-Bass, 2006), saying "that all are born 'in' and only some 'opt out.' " McKnight counters with this warning: "Any movement that is not evangelistic is failing the Lord."[9]

5. *Political*: "Tony Jones is regularly told that the emerging movement is a latte-drinking, backpack lugging, Birkenstock-wearing group of 21st-century, left-wing, hippie wannabes. Put directly, they are Democrats. And that spells 'post' for conservative-evangelical-politics as usual."[10]

Tom Sine has identified four major streams: emerging, missional, mosaic (ethnic and multicultural reaching out to a new generations), and monastic.[11] Mike Clawson provides a more extensive breakdown, expanding the list to ten and naming particular individuals and groups associated with each.

1. *Missional Church*: church as a missional community (David Bosch, Lesslie Newbigin)
2. *Ancient-Future Faith*: emphasis on reclaiming the rich worship resources of the ancient church (Robert Webber)

3. *Spiritual Formation*: emphasis on the regular practice of classic spiritual disciplines, both individually and in community (Richard Foster, Dallas Willard, Tony Jones, Gary Smalley)

4. *Alt. Worship*: creative, contextualized forms of worship; multisensory, techno-driven, and participatory (Dan Kimball,[12] Kester Brewin)

5. *Social Justice*: rediscovering the kingdom of God as a present reality in this world through creation care, racial reconciliation, economic justice, gender equality, liberation of the oppressed (Jim Wallis, Tony Campolo)

6. *New Monasticism*: pursuit of a simpler lifestyle, more holistic[13] (Shane Claiborne and the Simple Way community)

7. *Post-Liberal/Narrative Theology*: living into the biblical narrative rather than pegging faith to abstract propositions (Karl Barth, George Lindbeck, Hans Frei, Stanley Hauerwas, and William Willimon)

8. *Radical Orthodoxy*: outgrowth of narrative theology attempting to meld postmodern philosophy with historic Christian theology (John Milbank, James K. A. Smith, Catherine Pickstock, Ekklesia Project in Chicago)

9. *Post-Conservative Theology*: sees the theological task as a journey rather than arrival, which has a transformative impact (Stanley Grenz, Roger Olson, John Franke, N. T. Wright, Clark Pinnock, Greg Boyd, and William Dyrness)

10. *Post-Colonialism*: emergent church thinking in Africa, Latin America, and Southeast Asia that is developing contextualized theologies; prefer to use this term rather than "postmodern"[14] (Myra Rivera, Elizabeth Johnson, and Sharada Sugirtharajah)

Underlying each of the emergent streams is the recognition of a need for change. Some emphasize the need for theology to be liberated from its rationalist-modern construct, while others point to the fact that hierarchical and controlling church structures need to be replaced. Others want emergent to signify the planting of a new generation of churches whose heartbeat is mission, expressed in a holistic way, and who incorporate into their communal life a passion to make Jesus known and for the gospel of the kingdom to bring about a more just society. Still others take as their starting point the need for a new generation of leadership that operates in a non-controlling, empowering, and risk-taking manner.

The following represents my own attempt to provide some parameters to help determine the extent to which a church is both emerging and missional:

Internal focus	⟷	External focus
Inherited denomination	⟷	Independent network
Monocultural	⟷	Multicultural
Theologically conservative	⟷	Theologically liberal
Attractional	⟷	Missional
High-profile celebrity leader	⟷	Low-profile situational leader
Negative toward popular culture	⟷	Engaging popular culture

While the intention of this study is to identify and provide examples of the various streams, we pause to reflect on the courses that these various streams are taking. Will they continue to diverge, or will we see an increasing convergence? Phyllis Tickle, founding editor of the religion department of *Publishers Weekly*, opts for the latter scenario. In a talk she gave at the 2005 Emergent convention in Nashville, she represented the emerging church as a convergence of liturgical, evangelical, mainline, and Pentecostal elements. It seeks to find common ground and to promote a willingness, even eagerness, to learn from each other.[15] Tony Jones, national coordinator of Emergent Village, describes what is meant by "generous orthodoxy" when he says, "Emergents find little importance in the discrete differences between the various flavors of Christianity. Instead, they practice a generous orthodoxy that appreciates the contributions of all Christian movements."[16]

Mission Engagement As the Key Criterion

These lists demonstrate the complexity of the emerging church phenomenon, a complexity that is often overlooked by those critics who
tend to focus on the more questionable assertions, or speculations, of
a handful of spokespersons. They need, rather, to stand back and give
attention to the major concerns of emerging church leaders regarding
the failures of institutional Christianity and lack of cultural engagement, which have given rise to both the missional and emergent
initiatives. As we are here dealing with the morphing of the church
in order to engage the current missional challenges presented by
Western societies, we will focus on those streams that best represent
attempts to engage the culture with the gospel. In so doing, we may
discover that such engagement requires a major restructuring and
re-equipping of the church as we have known it.

3

fresh expressions

Most traditional denominations have come to realize that the leaders who are most committed to church planting are the ones experiencing growth at the present time. This can be seen, for example, among the Southern Baptists, the Churches of Christ, and the Nazarenes. When the newly planted, growing churches are analyzed, the majority of them represent initiatives in new or expanding suburbs or urban ministry among predominantly non-Caucasian communities, such as Hispanic, Korean, and Filipino. Church plants by traditional denominations among Caucasians in older neighborhoods are not faring as well. Most either remain small or fail to survive. This pattern holds true in North America as well as in Europe.[1]

I remember a church planting conference held in Nottingham, England, in 1995 that drew enthusiastic support from a wide range of denominations, including Anglicans, Methodists, Pentecostals, house church networks, and the Salvation Army. Unfortunately, the enthusiasm and optimism generated at that conference did not translate into a surge in church planting sufficient to reverse decades of decline. In the United States, denominational efforts have delivered similarly meager results.

Traditional denominations on both sides of the Atlantic suffer from a number of drawbacks. First, the model of church they are endeavoring to reproduce is a style of church shaped by and suited for Christendom; it is not a missional model. This reality becomes even more pronounced when members of the leadership core impose their preconceptions, drawn largely from the older, Christendom-shaped model, which quickly leaves the new churches locked into the past.

Second, the new church plants have to meet criteria set by the denomination in order to be considered a full-fledged church. This means that church planting becomes phenomenally expensive, as it is tied to real estate, meeting pay scales for professional clergy, and the purchase of furnishings. In the case of liturgical churches, vestments, altar adornments, and communion silverware are all part of the start-up costs.

Third, traditional denominations suffer from a shortage of trained and passionate church planters. They tend to attract and train leaders who look to the church to provide security and a career in ministry, rather than groundbreaking risk-takers.

Fourth, the seminaries that provide their leaders have trained their students in teaching and pastoring existing congregations, rather than in how to birth and reproduce new faith communities. Their curriculum is not designed to provide the necessary training for church planters. It is not denominational seminaries but Bible schools, parachurch agencies, and new apostolic networks that are most likely to design courses and provide boot camp–type experiences that will enable new church planters to interpret the social contexts in which they will be operating, build a team there, survive the first five years, and establish indigenous and reproducible models of church.

Fresh Expressions Envisioned by the Church of England

At long last, significant changes are now taking place among traditional denominations. Within the Church of England, a working group produced in 2003 a visionary report on church planting, which was published the following year under the title *Mission-Shaped Church*.[2] In 2005 it was in its seventh printing, which must be something of a record for a church report! This 174-page book is now available online.[3] In 2004 the general synod of the Church of England commended the report to the whole church for study and implementation, and Steven Croft was appointed as Archbishops' Missioner and Team Leader of the Fresh Expressions initiative.

The report stresses that church planting should not be regarded as an end in itself, but rather as a God-ordained means by which the reign of God on earth is extended. Not that the church is itself the kingdom, but rather that it is a sign and anticipation of the universal reign of God. Church planting must not be adopted as a strategy to ensure institutional survival but as a way to multiply faith communities that witness, in word and deed, to the transforming power of the gospel.

> For Anglican Christians God's mission is about transformation— transforming individual lives, transforming communities and transforming the world. As we follow Jesus Christ, we believe that God's mission is revealed to us by the Holy Spirit in three ways: through the Bible, through the tradition and life of the Church, and through our own listening, praying, thinking and sharing as we respond to our own context.[4]

Fresh expressions of church are intended to manifest the "Five Marks of Mission," a document adopted by the Lambeth Conference in 1988 and affirmed by the Church of England in 1996. These five marks are:

1. To proclaim the good news of the kingdom
2. To teach, baptize, and nurture new believers
3. To respond to human need by loving service
4. To seek to transform unjust structures of society
5. To strive to safeguard the integrity of creation and to sustain the life of the earth[5]

Building on these five marks of mission, *Mission-Shaped Church* speaks of five values for a missionary church:

1. "A missionary church is focused on God the Trinity. . . . Worship lies at the heart of a missionary church, and to love and know God as Father, Son and Spirit is its chief inspiration and primary purpose."
2. "A missionary church is incarnational. . . . [It] seeks to shape itself in relation to the culture in which it is located or to which it is called."
3. "A missionary church is transformational. . . . [It] exists for the transformation of the community that it serves, through the power of the gospel and the Holy Spirit."
4. "A missionary church makes disciples. . . . [It] is active in calling people to faith in Jesus Christ. . . . It is concerned for the transformation of individuals, as well as for the transformation of communities."
5. "A missionary church is relational. . . . It is characterized by welcome and hospitality. Its ethos and style are open to change when new members join."[6]

To these five values, I would add two more: First, a missionary church is reproducible. By this I mean that new faith communities are produced, not simply carbon copies of the mother church. The genius of the early church arose from the fact that each faith community had within itself, in reliance on the equipping and guidance of the Holy Spirit, all the necessary resources to give birth to new faith communities. Herein lies a continuing blind spot in the vision of traditional denominations, due in part to their hierarchical straitjacket. The assumption prevails that significant initiatives invariably begin at the top level of decision-makers and from there percolate down to the grass roots. But the history of mission tells a different story, with initiatives often begun at the ground level by individuals and small groups, motivated by a God-given vision.

The second value I would add is that a missionary church combines local engagement with global concerns and commitment. The Great Commission challenges every faith community to begin with its local context, and then to see beyond its immediate context to the peoples of the world, both near and far. In other words, it must not become so immersed in its local context that it fails to see beyond it. While mission begins with our "Jerusalem," it also extends to the ends of the earth.

Fresh Expressions recognizes that a changing social context, resulting in the increased marginalization of the church, has necessitated alternative forms of church. These will be distinct from the parochial model that has prevailed throughout England and in most of Europe. In his introduction to the report, Graham Cray, bishop of Maidstone, who served as chairman of the working group, writes:

> We understand "church planting" to refer to the discipline of "creating new communities of Christian faith as part of the mission of God to express God's kingdom in every geographic and cultural context." "Fresh expressions of church" are manifestations of this, but they also give evidence of many parishes' attempts to make a transition into a more missional form of church.[7]

It recognizes that Britain is now a post-Christian society that has bypassed the influence of the institutional church in redefining its core identity. Changing social mores reflect the progressive influence of secularization, pluralism, and relativism. The parochial system is crumbling, due to shrinking local pools of support, and its approach has become too static for a mobile and fragmented society. It therefore needs to be complemented by more innovative and experimental forms of Christian community. The report identifies fresh expressions of church that "are connecting with people through the networks in which they live, rather than through the place where they live."[8] It also seeks to establish a mutual partnership between parochial and network churches, rather than setting them in a competing relationship, resulting in one growing at the expense of the other.

The disappointing results of denominational church planting efforts in the preceding fifteen years have made it clear that church planting must not be construed as church cloning. The problem with the image of planting is that it suggests a predetermined model that will be inserted into a host culture, without regard for its relevance. In order to avoid this impression, I personally prefer the language of birthing, which emphasizes that a new church is not simply the latest model of an already-existing church, but rather represents a newly created church that is birthed within specific cultural contexts. It is not simply new in time, but new in concept. The *Mission-Shaped Church* report highlights this key understanding in bold type:

> The planting process is the engagement of church and gospel with a new mission context, and this should determine the fresh expression of church.[9]

Furthermore, fresh expressions are not simply shop windows or halfway houses, designed to provide an introductory experience of church for those alienated from traditional church life. They are not created with the intention of establishing temporary faith communities that will transfer later to the real thing. To the contrary, they are themselves authentic expressions of church that are indigenous to their cultural contexts, the contexts in which they exercise a missional calling. This entails a discerning cultural appreciation, as well as a willingness to submit to the critique of the gospel, both with a view to community transformation.

Two aspects of the report are particularly refreshing: first, its ecumenical spirit. It draws from the insights and experience of a wide variety of church planting endeavors from other historic denominations as well as from independent networks. Second, it reaches beyond Europe to gain from the insights of the growing churches in the Global South. The report recognizes that the church in England is enriched by a two-way traffic: of English Christians visiting the worldwide church, and of Christians from other parts of the world bringing their spiritual exuberance to a jaded Western church. Their different ways of doing things stimulate the imagination of Western Christians, helping them face their shortcomings. The report acknowledges the contribution that many Anglican mission agencies are now making as they work to enhance the mission impetus of the church in England, in response to its domestic mission challenges.[10]

As I was working on this chapter, I came across an inspiring example of the unintentional birthing of a faith community in Cambridgeshire, England, where a couple birthed a house church with the aim of evangelizing their local community.[11] Their outreach in the town center was held in a bus, which attracted the interest of two women with learning disabilities. The women invited others from their network. The group began meeting with the leaders, Edward and Marilyn Kerr, with the permission of their caregivers and home managers. Up to thirty-five people, including the caregivers, now meet three Sundays a month in a local scout hall. In addition, the Kerrs open their home once a month for a prayer meeting and holding monthly meetings in six residential care homes.

This outcome was very different from the original vision the Kerrs had when they set out to evangelize the local community. They have been on a steep learning curve, not having had previous experience of ministry among people with learning disabilities. They have drawn on the resources of Causeway Prospects, an organization that offers training and advice in support of churches doing ministry among people with learning disabilities.[12] What the congregation lacks in verbal skills they make up for in other ways: by playing percussion instruments and waving flags, for example. The Kerrs report that one young man with Down Syndrome, "who rarely talks and can sign only badly, is wonderfully sensitive with flags, waving them over the congregation in a way that's very prophetic and moving."[13]

The term "Fresh Expressions" was adopted in the Church of England to suggest that "something new or enlivening is happening, but also suggests connection to history and the developing story of God's work in the church."[14] It expresses the idea of "emergence" while providing distance from the baggage that term has gathered in recent years. The plural form "fresh expressions" also recognizes the diversity of models emerging according to the context and calling of each faith community. The *Mission-Shaped Church* report provides examples to illustrate the range of expressions.

It is one thing to declare a strategy, but its implementation is another matter. Often in the past, church reports have led to much being said while little is done. Fortunately, this has not been the case with Fresh Expressions, as there are numerous examples of words being translated into action, including a UK-based newspaper called "Expressions" and a Web site that gives schedules of courses available around the country, along with news that is updated monthly.[15] A range of training opportunities are also available around the country, including vision days arranged by Fresh Expressions; a six-week introductory course on becoming a mission-shaped church; and a one-year mission-shaped ministry course. Fresh Expressions also partners with other organizations offering courses and conferences.

Across the Atlantic in both Canada and the United States, interest in this UK initiative is awakening. *Quadrant*, the bimonthly bulletin of research-based information produced by Christian Research, UK, reports that in 2008 "there are some 5,000 examples [of fresh expressions] in the Church of England alone. At least some, though almost certainly not all, of these people will be new to church attendance or membership, so their numbers are very likely to have a significant impact on overall numbers in the years ahead."[16]

We must, however, add a cautionary word in recognition of the fact that we are speaking of a recent and developing phenomenon. Time alone will tell how many of these fresh expressions will eventually fade, wilt, and die. Each fresh expression will require careful nurturing through the availability of training resources, pastoral support of initiative-taking leaders, and a willingness on the part of leaders to make themselves accountable to coaches and peer mentors.

With so many fresh expressions of church now in place alongside existing congregations, the time is ripe for the joint, grassroots initiative called Hope 2008 that combines worship, social action, and evangelism.[17] Hope 2008 has been generating interest and gathering momentum across the United Kingdom. It is sponsored by major denominations and independent networks, along with youth outreach agencies, such as Youth for Christ, and other evangelistic movements. This kind of widespread cooperation and commitment to a common vision, both at the grassroots level and from the national leadership of churches and agencies, is refreshing to see. Chapter 5 will offer a fuller discussion of the Hope 2008 initiative and other similar cooperative movements.

A number of prominent church leaders and institutions are taking the lead in the implementation of Fresh Expressions. As we have already mentioned, the archbishop of Canterbury appointed Steven Croft to lead Fresh Expressions teams in 2004. George Lings, who directs the highly regarded Sheffield Centre, uses case study research to provide expertise in discerning the evolving mission of the church. Some of the key questions addressed in their research are: "Who is intentionally working among the non-churched? What works in mission that goes beyond the fringe? And what ways of being church will grow in response?"[18]

In addition, Reverend Bob Hopkins, who was a consulting editor with the team that produced the *Mission-Shaped Church*, and his wife Mary are also in Sheffield and are pioneering Anglican Church Planting Initiatives (ACPI). ACPI exists to " 'serve tomorrow's churches today' by encouraging and assisting the planting of healthy, missionary-minded churches. [They] are a small charity, but with a committed central team and a large national network, working with churches and people called to church planting, fresh expressions of church and multiplying communities of mission." They work

1. Primarily within the Anglican Church but also with the wider church
2. To serve the vision of creating new communities of faith as part of the mission of God to express the Gospel of Jesus Christ and His Kingdom in every geographic and cultural context
3. To promote the necessary institutional developments to facilitate this

To this end, ACPI offers the following services:

1. Provide advice, coaching and consultancy to Anglicans (and other denominations and streams when time permits) on Planting Churches, fresh expressions, mission projects, church growth and leadership . . .
2. Supply resources on Church Planting and Cell Church, including training workbooks, books and other literature
3. Arrange various conferences and training courses on Church Planting and missional leadership
4. Have a training course called "Planting Healthy Churches" which can be run to support a number of church plant teams in an area[19]

In addition to providing these services, ACPI works in partnership with the Sheffield Centre, a research unit sponsored by the Church Army, to refer churches and individuals to Anglican Church Plants and other projects that are nearby.

The Fresh Expressions initiative has studiously avoided a centralized, bureaucratic approach. Instead it has forged a coalition of agencies working together, each contributing from their store of expertise.

North American Churches' Response to the Call to Mission

In the United States most traditional denominations have a church growth division within their home mission department. Each tends to work independently of other denominations, because their own "tribe" provides the needed resources and finds itself in a competitive relationship with other denominations, church planting movements, and consulting agencies. Distance also contributes to a lack of cooperation, along with the fact that in many areas of the country there are a plethora of traditions, with no principal denomination or extensive network taking the lead or bringing others around itself cooperatively.

But the absence of an overall strategy is not simply explained by the geographic size of the United States in comparison to England. Canada, for instance, has organized a number of national church planting conferences that embrace a wide variety of denominations and traditions. The vision of Church Planting Canada, for example, is that every neighborhood would be "transformed through the presence of multiplying missional communities incarnating the gospel."[20] In pursuit of that vision, it has organized a national congress every two years since 1997.

Although Canada is further along the path to secularization than the United States, both have to address the challenge of the nature of the church in post-Christendom contexts. The majority of denominational church planting initiatives consist of attempts to work according to existing templates. Slowly, the realization is dawning of the need to birth new kinds of church, instead of attempting to multiply existing models. On more than one occasion, after addressing leaders in a traditional denomination, I have heard concerns expressed as to whether the new faith communities emerging within traditional denominations are *really* Presbyterian, Lutheran, Episcopal, or whatever the tradition in question.

One leader of the home missions department of his denomination confessed to me that the innovative new church plants could not obtain a pin number to be properly registered because they did not meet his denomination's criteria! Perplexed leaders need to distinguish between the treasure of their tradition and the baggage they carry along with it. Loyalty to tradition does not consist in living in the past but in learning from the past, and in reinterpreting the tradition in light of a changing social context.

I have also detected a tendency for many emerging churches to move in an Anabaptist direction. This trend reflects their leaders' concerns that churches had been subverted, under the influence of Christendom, by the pervasive impact of the culture and the agendas of political parties. This trend is more marked in England and Canada than it is in the United States.[21] Despite the efforts of the missional church and emerging church conversations, the challenge remains to integrate ecclesiology and missiology. Contemporary expressions of church, as well as historic churches, need to be liberated from their Christendom paradigm and the subversion of consumerism.

Traditional Denominations in the United States

Any account of the rise of emerging churches within historic denominations in the United States must begin with the vision and ministry of Karen Ward in Seattle. She is an African American who served for a number of years at the headquarters of the Evangelical Lutheran Church of America. She is credited with naming the emerging church movement through her Web site of that name, launched in 2000. In 2002 she founded the Church of the Apostles, which is both Lutheran and Episcopalian.[22] This emerging church seeks to embody the radical emphasis in Luther's doctrine of the priesthood of all believers.

This is what worship at this "emergent" congregation looks like, as participants light candles during a sanctorum service. In liturgy and theology we are "1,000 percent Lutheran," said Karen Ward, pastor, who came to Seattle three years ago to develop Church of the Apostles.

Being Lutheran includes what Ward called a "radical inhabitation of [Martin] Luther's 'priesthood of all believers.' " That plays out here with leadership of the more than 60 members who understand themselves to be "a radically practicing community of baptismally ordained priests." Ward said this community connects with people who say they are "spiritual but church wary."[23]

Fremont Abbey in Seattle is a further expression of Karen Ward's vision. It was opened in January 2007 with the following vision statement,

The Fremont Abbey Arts Center strives to be a "third place" within the community, providing a welcoming space beyond work and home to gather with others for performances, workshops, collaboration and classes. The Abbey aims to host diverse arts education programs with our focus on music, visual, and literary arts for youth and adults residing especially in Fremont and North Seattle. Our desire is to help people from all walks of life and income levels to learn and develop through experiences with the arts.[24]

A new blog called "Reformergent" seeks to find common ground between Reformed theology and the emerging church, focusing mainly on theological interaction rather than on church planting initiatives. In response to online comments about the emerging church by Rick McKinley of the Imago Dei community in Portland, Reformergent blogger Chris Case agrees with McKinley's portrayal of "the desire people often have to place people instantly into 'categories' to decide whether we agree with them or don't, often without delving into their writings or work." Case continues, "I think there are individuals in the Reformed or conservative camps who instantly label emerging folks as liberal or unorthodox. Individuals within the emerging movement also instantly label its critics as 'modern' and not 'forward-thinking' just because they disagree with where they perceive the emerging church [to be] headed."[25] Case expresses his qualified support of the emerging movement, respectful of the fact that God is doing a new thing, while at the same time feeling that the biblical hermeneutic of some of its leaders raises serious concerns.

The "Presbymergent" Web site is another online home for dialogue, one that is attracting increasing attention. Its primary aim is not to save the Presbyterian church, but simply to engage with attempts to address the current missional challenges facing the church. As one Presbymergent contributor puts it, "I am not interested in 'saving' the Presbyterian Church (USA). What I am interested in is the kingdom of God—I am interested in helping others find ways in which they can live out their faith, and find the ways in which they can participate in the hopes and dreams of God. I think both Emergent and the Presbyterian Church can contribute to those goals."[26]

The Presbyterian Church (USA) has recently begun funding emerging Presbyterian churches through grants related to specific projects. A grant given to The Open Door, an emerging Presbyterian church in Pittsburgh, pastored by B. J. Woodworth, is to be used "to help them assess the needs within their lower-income and culturally diverse neighborhoods; conduct surveys and meet neighbors in hopes [of learning] their stories; research, train and develop strategies for becoming the multicultural church they hope to be; hire an intern (for two consecutive years) to work with their church in building bridges with minority populations in their urban neighborhood and developing indigenous leaders from the neighborhood." A second grant was awarded to The Living Room, an emerging Presbyterian church in the Westside neighborhood of Atlanta, pastored by Tom Livengood, to help fund the development of their Web site and "virtual community," for which they will partner with a local advertising firm.[27]

David T. Olson, director of the American Church Research Project and director of church planting for the Evangelical Covenant Church (ECC), informed me that his denomination is trying to do a small number of "controlled experiments" with edgy models of church each year. He gives as examples a monastic church plant and a version of a "multiple house church" that meets once a month. He also reported that "their strongest area of church planting right now is intentional multiethnic church plants. The ECC has twelve exceptionally gifted non-Anglo church planters doing this. There are very few 'intentional' multiethnic church plants in the whole country that are strong in theological and sociological foundations."[28]

The North American Baptists have an active church planting initiative, including an annual conference that, when it was addressed in 2008 by Neil Cole of Church Multiplication Associates, was advertised as follows:

> Don't just plant a church, start a community. Go beyond the hype and clever marketing of the consumer-driven church, and partner with Jesus in building the organic body of Christ. *The Quest* gives the planter and their core community the tools they need to get the job done. This three-day intensive is non-model specific, culturally neutral and driven by principles derived directly from the ministry model of Jesus.[29]

Rick Mysse consults with a number of denominations committed to planting reproducing churches in Southern California. In the past, he has worked with the Assemblies of God, the Vineyard, and the Reformed Church in America. He currently works with over sixty congregations.

The Anglican Communion Network is an association of over nine hundred theologically conservative congregations across the United States working for renewal. Reverend Tom Herrick serves as their national director for church planting, working to set up regional church planting networks.[30]

Within the Nazarene denomination, Mike Williams, director of church relations at Mount Vernon Christian University, is mentoring a group of young pastors in Ohio who are pioneering innovative approaches through their LEAP program, which offers seminars in the areas of leadership, evangelism, administration, and preaching/worship.[31]

Independent Initiatives within the United States

Given the entrepreneurial nature of the culture and a tradition of local church independence within the United States, most fresh expressions of church occur as local initiatives, rather than as the outcomes of centralized planning at the denominational level.

• Jacob's Well (Kansas City, Missouri) •

Fresh expressions of church in North America arise in a variety of ways. Some are the result of individuals and groups becoming dissatisfied with their megachurch experience. Tim Keel, the founding pastor at Jacob's Well, is a case in point. He says, "My former church was a suburban megachurch functioning under Willow Creek's seeker-targeted church paradigm. I was a naive and idealistic twenty-seven-year-old wanting to call off all bets in order to creatively engage everything in the pursuit of God."[32]

Keel's book *Intuitive Leadership* does not offer a prescription for successful leadership. Rather, it is an account of the author's spiritual pilgrimage; his experience of in-depth fellowship in the college community; his confusion arising from his seminary experience; and his founding of Jacob's Well in Kansas City. The author offers no model of how to do church. Instead he emphasizes the need to listen to the voices around you in order to interpret the context. Leadership is intuitive and not prescribed.

In the church's own words,

> Jacob's Well began with a handful of people in 1998. We are joined together around a dream and a call from God to build a community in midtown Kansas City with Jesus Christ at the center. Our desire is that we would be an authentic biblical community where people experience and express the reality of God's love in the way of Jesus. Our name [recalls Jesus' encounter with] a woman who is at the fringes of her culture, a woman with great hunger and great need. Jesus reaches out to her and invites her into his life and kingdom. . . . Jacob's Well is striving to be a place—like the biblical Jacob's Well—where people who are searching can encounter God and find a place in his kingdom and community and join him in his work in the world.[33]

The people of Jacob's Well spell out their vision in terms of the biblical narrative they seek to make their own, in order to make it known to the surrounding community.

> We believe that any community calling itself a church lives in the tension between two realities. Our community is a part of the larger story of God's activity in the world. Our church revolves around the story of God and his people found in our scriptures, the Bible. We are biblical—we live and struggle within the boundaries the scriptures give us. We are also authentic. We believe that God is honored and lives are transformed when people are honest, genuine, and real, exposing their brokenness to God and to others. We try not to wear masks. We believe that living the tension of being biblically-based *and* authentic is a challenge, but one that is incredibly exciting and life-giving.
>
> What is the response of this community to God's reality present in our midst? We believe it is a two-fold response. We are invited to experience the reality of God's love for us in our own lives. We are invited to worship God, to grow in our knowledge and obedience to him, to experience his presence in our community. But it doesn't end there. God's life is not given for merely selfish reasons. We are also invited to express God's love in the world in real, tangible ways, and to share what we know about Jesus with those who do not know him. Christianity is a way of life that sends us into the world to serve God and our neighbors so that God's will is done on earth as it is in heaven. The church is never to be a withdrawn, isolated end user of the gospel of Jesus; rather, we receive it so that we may be equipped and sent into the world to love our neighbors and serve "the least of these." In this sense, Jacob's Well doesn't *have* a mission; *it is* mission.[34]

In keeping with many churches that are committed to reaching out to their generation, they "are a church where people are allowed to belong before they believe, where people are listened to, not preached at." They seek to create a space "where it is safe to share doubts and questions, struggles . . . and pain, along with fun and parties."[35] They, like so many other emerging churches committed to mission, see themselves as being on a journey in which they invite others to share and discover alongside them.

• Dieter Zander's Pilgrimage •

Dieter Zander comes out of the conservative Baptist tradition. He was challenged to begin a new church that would reach out to young people, incorporating a rock band and drama into their worship. In 1984 he started NewSong Church in Upland (located today in San Dimas in Southern California).[36] The church grew from one hundred to twelve hundred in three years. They reached out to dissatisfied churchgoers, providing an alternative to the sort of polished per-formance, good-looking super pastor that typically appealed to the Boomer generation. Zander writes, "We wanted to show dirt, and we included many types of people, not just professionals. We liked to celebrate. We were authentic but safe as well. We were rousing, real, relevant, and relational."[37] "NewSong takes its name and mission from Psalm 40:1–3: 'I waited patiently for the LORD; he turned to me and heard my cry. He lifted me out of the slimy pit, out of the mud and mire; he set my feet on a rock and gave me a firm place to stand. He put a new song in my mouth, a hymn of praise to our God. Many will see and fear and put their trust in the LORD.'"[38]

In January 1994 Dieter Zander left NewSong to develop a Generation X ministry at Willow Creek called "Axis." Eventually, a difference of opinion arose between Zander and Bill Hybels around the question of whether the Axis ministry represented a transitional phase for de-churched emerging adults or whether it was an alternative expression of church that pointed to the future. In 1998 Zander and his wife took a five-month sabbatical, which led to their move to San Francisco, where they began working with Mark Scandrette and others to develop a community that sought "to reimagine what life with God might look like in real practical terms."[39] He is currently the pastor of arts and spiritual formation—a missionary in residence—at BayMarin Church, north of San Francisco, in a county that has one of the lowest rates of church attendance in the country.[40]

• Solomon's Porch (Minneapolis, Minnesota) •

Doug Pagitt began Solomon's Porch in 2000. The church's Web site states its mission in the following terms:

Solomon's Porch is a community seeking to live the dreams and love of God in the way of Jesus. . . . While we use our facility for Sunday evening worship gatherings, Bible studies, meals, [an] internet café, art exhibitions, and events, we are very aware that our community exists wherever the people of Solomon's Porch find themselves. In this way, our Christian lives are not limited to what we officially do in our meeting space, but are expressed through our lives.

We are seeking to be a redemptive, transformative community living as a blessing of God in all the world. The people of our community are from varied backgrounds and perspectives, but find unity and commonality in seeking the things of God in this world, "as they are in heaven," in the generous Orthodox expressions of Christianity.[41]

In this description we see some familiar themes that are characteristic of those churches within the emergent stream that demonstrate a commitment to holistic mission. Solomon's Porch is seeking to live out a radical expression of the gospel, identifying with "the way of Jesus." It is Jesus who provides the model, the inspiration, and the power (John 17:18; 20:21). They think of church as much more than a weekly gathering. It is an ongoing community in which people find identity in service, offering hospitality to all. Their worship includes the offering of the creative expressions with which the members are endowed. They are committed to service in their neighborhoods to bring about transformation. And their total ministry is inspired by their interaction with the Scriptures.

• Mars Hill (Grandville, Michigan) •

Rob Bell, who has achieved a high media profile, is pastor of Mars Hill, a church that is rooted in the orthodox Christian faith, while constantly exploring, believing that the church is on a journey as it seeks to live out God's future. It rejects the split between the sacred and the secular, believing that "God wants to bring about a new humanity by redeeming every part of us." It seeks to live in authentic community, praying for one another and bearing each other's burdens. It challenges the individualism of Western culture, with the conviction that "the way of Jesus cannot be lived alone." It is committed to serving, "passionate about relieving suffering and fighting injustice." And the people of Mars Hill see life as celebration: "We take great joy in partnering with God to change the world, embracing the truth that all of life is sacred, hope is real and tomorrow can be better than today. We celebrate the divine in the daily, pursuing lives of hope, gratitude, and worship."[42]

• Vintage Faith Church (Santa Cruz, California) •

Dan Kimball is an acknowledged leader in the emerging church stream and is pastor of Vintage Faith Church, a church that places a strong emphasis on worship, which it expresses in a variety of ways, recognizing that people have a diversity of learning styles and temperaments. Vintage Faith Church is creative in its approach to worship, out of the conviction that each person is created to reflect the image of God, who is the ultimate Creator. To develop this conviction, they have formed a community for those interested in art, music, theater, and film. Their worship style is a blend of ancient and present, drawing upon the rich tradition of Christian worship throughout past centuries, while seeking and relying upon the guidance of the Holy Spirit rather than by depending on human know-how.

In keeping with the other models mentioned in this section, Vintage Faith Church is also dispersed throughout the surrounding area through community groups, which are not just home meetings but mini-churches; they study, pray, and "do life" together. In addition, they have an expanding range of affinity groups: for example, outdoor adventurers, ministry to women, artists, etc. Their community life is not *at the expense of* mission, but rather *an expression of* mission. They write, "We will take the commands of Jesus seriously and do whatever it takes to see others experience the Kingdom of God and the good news of Jesus."[43] The community groups seek to relate to their cultural context without conforming to it. They passionately seek to reach out to those who have rejected the Christian faith, in order that they might experience the light and love of Jesus through the welcoming faith community. And they see missions holistically, both local and global, and involving issues of justice.

Fresh Expressions within Canadian Denominations

Cam Roxburgh wears a number of hats, serving as senior pastor of
Southside Community Church, as well as national director of Church
Planting Canada and missional director for Canadian Baptist Ministries, and the national director of the Missional Training Network
(MTN) in Canada. One of his team members, Terry Crowley, serves
as MTN's Emerging Generation Facilitator. He is working hard with
Mark Anderson of Youth for Christ (YFC) to create a leadership
program for the emerging generation. As we might expect, there
is a strong youth emphasis in churches planted by YFC ministries,
such as Station X and Warehouse 180, led by Andy Harrington, a
YFC leader from the United Kingdom.

Following the MTN Conference in 2003, in which I was privileged to participate, Cam asked, "What do you get when you put
656 denominational leaders, pastors, church planters, intercessors
and other interested parties into the intimate setting of First Baptist
Church, Vancouver?" (which hosted the conference). This is how he
responds to his own question:

> You get a glimpse into a momentum-gathering movement of God's
> people that is indicative of what God has in store for the church
> across Canada.... I believe there are signs of it [i.e., church planting]
> becoming a priority right across this land.
>
> As the church in Canada continues to be marginalized, believ-
> ers are realizing that there needs to be a recommitment to being
> the people of God in the midst of neighbourhoods—in order to
> glorify God by reaching our friends with the good news of Christ.
> Church planting is an excellent tool of the Kingdom, that fosters
> the work of the Spirit in the context of a world heading in the op-
> posite direction.
>
> As we dreamed and prayed about what God wanted to do at the
> Congress in Vancouver, we became aware of all kinds of questions and
> not a whole lot of answers. Hence, the title: "Next . . . ?" Our desire
> was to help people to break out of their comfort zones by raising
> questions that would leave us gasping for breath and turning to the
> Lord, first in repentance and then for direction. For too long, we as
> the church have done things in our own strength. It is time to lay

down the plans for the church we are trying to recapture and pick up the blueprints for the church that God has in mind.[44]

• Southside Community Church •
(Vancouver, British Columbia)

Cam Roxburgh's work is grounded in his own experience as a church planter working in one of the most deprived neighborhoods in Vancouver. Southside Community Church is now distributed among four congregations spread across the city. They are committed to keeping congregations small enough so that people can get to know one another and challenge each other to live a life of deeper discipleship. A decentralized approach also enables them to reach into their neighborhoods so that the life of the faith community can spill into the surrounding area.

Their decentralized approach also creates the need for a growing pool of leadership. Small-scale events encourage emerging leaders to develop their talents and confidence and give them opportunities to build upon their experience in serving the various congregations. Southside Community Church also recognizes the value of bringing the congregations together for joint celebration, as well as expanding the vision to reach not only Vancouver and British Columbia, but across the nation and even the world.[45]

• Ecclesiax (Ottawa, Ontario) •

Ecclesiax is a Free Methodist church ministering among the artistic community of Ottawa. Joseph Anthony Moreau describes himself as "point leader and communicator." The church advertises its Sunday services as a "Worship Palette," which is "a crazy God encounter through art, music, sacred readings, God stories, wine and bread." They are "a community of people that have heard God, fallen in love with Him, and are obedient to Him. A community motivated by the heartbeat of God, which is burning with freedom, passion, beauty, creativity, and the source of all life. A community that is serious about helping people connect with their God dream." They are missional in their commitment, finding people who will, in turn, reproduce Christ-followers. In keeping with other examples provided in this chapter, "they see themselves as within an ancient tradition. Ecclesiax is not a new idea, it is just going back to the beginning."[46]

The church expresses a strong commitment to community in the following terms:

> *Freedom*—Allow each person to uniquely experience freedom in God.
> *Embracing*—You will be accepted as you are.
> *Accountability*—Relationships require effort, which is key to community.
> *Sacrificial*—We give of our time, resources, talents, until it hurts.
> *Authenticity*—Honesty about ourselves is essential, although sometimes frightening.
> *Forgiveness*—We forgive because we've been forgiven.
> *Transformational*—Community has the power to impact people's lives.

When I met Joseph while leading a session for the Arrow Leadership Program, he told me the story of a well-known Canadian sculptor who had begun to attend Ecclesiax. Although not yet a believer, he gave a double tithe to the church. One day he said to Joseph, "I think Jesus was the greatest con artist who ever lived." The pastor's response was, "Could we place that opinion on a sign outside the church?" "Sure," the sculptor responded. "But I'd want to make one change," Joseph continued. "I want to place a question mark after your statement!"

Summary

The purpose of this chapter has been to provide a wide range of illustrations to indicate that emerging missional initiatives are by no means confined to breakaway or independent groups. I believe there is mounting evidence to demonstrate that some of the most innovative, and potentially most enduring and significant, "fresh expressions" of church are found within the inherited denominations. I say this because they have the potential to influence the traditions that have birthed them, helping them transition from their Christendom mindset to engage the missional challenges of a post-secular society. These ancient traditions in themselves contain elements that are being discovered by a new generation of faith communities that are seeking to be enriched by the experience and insight of the generations of believers in Christ that preceded them.

For their part, the new networks of churches also have much to contribute to the debate, because they have the freedom to innovate and take risks. They are liberated from the institutional controls that can frustrate and shackle a new generation of leaders. These emerging leaders need trust and freedom to "travel light," in order to birth new faith communities in large and growing segments of the population that are beyond the reach of institutional religion. Alongside them, leaders within the new independent networks (which we will explore further in chapter 7) can provide encouragement and fresh experimental models by reaching out to those pioneers who remain loyal to their inherited traditions. Likewise, those within the inherited traditions can provide historical perspective and a broader frame of reference, which will help the freewheeling entrepreneurs learn from the failed attempts and deviant movements that litter the pages of church history.

Whether emerging churches represent the morphing of long-established traditions or the birthing of entirely new movements, one of the greatest challenges they all face is that of the urban world and the cultures it forges that have a profound and pervasive global impact. In chapter 5 we will see indications of a renewed realization of the importance of the city and a fresh sense of call to engage the urban challenge, as evidenced in the lives of many younger leaders.

_ _4_ _ _ _ _ _

the megachurch factor

The role of megachurches in relation to the emerging church phenomenon is potentially of great significance. This arises, not only because of the size of these churches and their increasing number, but also because of their influence, both nationally and internationally. They maintain a high profile through their publishing, leadership conferences, and associations of churches that look to them for inspiration and resources.

Until recently, it was widely assumed that megachurches were antithetical to the emerging churches' understanding of church. This had to do primarily with the stance of most megachurches as attractional rather than incarnational, and consumerist rather than participatory. But now all that is beginning to change, with some prominent megachurches reassessing their strategies, seeing themselves playing a role within a larger missional movement. They are not only contributing from their own resources but learning from the experience of smaller, reproducible faith communities that adapt to their local contexts.

The Strategic Importance of Megachurches

An extensive survey conducted by Leadership Network, entitled "Megachurches Today 2005," revealed that at the time of the survey there were at least 1,210 churches with weekly average attendances of over 2,000, which represents an increase of 100 percent within just five years.[1] Furthermore, there is no sign yet of that number having peaked. As Dave Travis, executive vice president of Leadership Network, points out, "During 2005 alone, four megachurch pastors had books on the *New York Times* bestseller lists," one significant indication of their wide-ranging influence. Their political importance, likewise, has not been overlooked in the run-up to the 2008 presidential election, with the *CQ Researcher* dedicating an entire issue to the "Rise of Megachurches."[2]

A number of myths have grown up around the megachurch phenomenon, eleven of which have been debunked by the "Megachurches Today 2005" survey:

MYTH #1: All megachurches are alike.
REALITY: They differ in growth rates, size and emphasis.

MYTH #2: All megachurches are equally good at being big.
REALITY: Some clearly understand how to function as a large institution, but others flounder.

MYTH #3: There is an over-emphasis on money in the megachurches.
REALITY: The data disputes this.

MYTH #4: Megachurches exist for spectator worship and are not serious about Christianity.
REALITY: Megachurches generally have high spiritual expectations and serious orthodox beliefs.

MYTH #5: Megachurches are not deeply involved in social ministry.
REALITY: Considerable ministry is taking place at and through these churches.

MYTH #6: All megachurches are pawns of or powerbrokers to George Bush and the Republican Party.
REALITY: The vast majority of megachurches are not politically active.

MYTH #7: All megachurches have huge sanctuaries and enormous campuses.
REALITY: Megachurches make widespread use of multiple worship services over several days, multiple venues, and even multiple campuses.

MYTH #8: All megachurches are nondenominational.
REALITY: The vast majority belong to some denomination.

MYTH #9: All megachurches are homogeneous congregations with little diversity.
REALITY: A large and growing number are multi-ethnic and intentionally so.

MYTH #10: Megachurches grow primarily because of great programming.
REALITY: Megachurches grow because excited attendees tell their friends.

MYTH #11: The megachurch phenomenon is on the decline.
REALITY: The data suggests that many more megachurches are on the way.[3]

However, one must not overlook the fact that less than 0.3 percent of churches fall into this category.[4] The assumptions megachurches make, as well as the strategies they choose to adopt, are not always readily transferable to the vast majority of churches with average weekly attendances of less than one hundred.[5] Furthermore, reliable field research needs to be undertaken to test the frequently made claim that megachurches are heavily dependent on feeder systems provided by smaller churches in their catchment area. In other words, is their growth largely the result of transfer of members and attendees from elsewhere, or are they attracting back to church significant numbers of people who had ceased to attend due to boredom or disillusionment?

We must also bear in mind that the traffic flow is not all one way. For instance, Bill Donahue, the executive director of Small Group Ministries Movement, reported to the author that Willow Creek sees more movement from Willow Creek to smaller churches than the reverse. This two-way traffic reflects the findings of the Pew Forum on Religion & Public Life survey of 35,000 adults, released in February 2008, which documents a religious population that is both diverse and dynamic, with significant numbers of people moving from one stream or denomination of Protestantism to another.[6]

A further factor to bear in mind when considering the continuing growth of megachurches is that many are located in newer suburban developments, or within easy freeway access to these new populations. Assuming that a significant percentage of the residents in these developments were church attendees in their previous location and that many did not have a strong denominational affiliation, some churches likely became megachurches largely because these residents went church shopping in their area. A strategic location is not the only growth factor. Church shoppers are especially drawn to churches that already have a high media profile, a reputation for high quality contemporary worship, and programs to meet the needs of young families. But sheer size can also prove intimidating to some people who assume that such mammoth churches are inevitably impersonal.

The fact is that not all megachurches are alike, as the Leadership Network study highlights. Some know how to function effectively as large institutions, while others do not. A healthy megachurch is not just successful at attracting a crowd, but also knows how to effectively enfold people into relational groups where they can grow to spiritual maturity. Many megachurches exert a wide influence through their television and radio programs, podcasts, leadership seminars providing inspiration and training for church leaders, and through the printed and DVD program resources that they produce and distribute.

Within the United Kingdom, Peter Brierley's 2005 research also draws attention to the increasing significance of the larger Church of England churches.[7] The growing churches are either large or have congregations of less than 50 members; churches in the middle zone, with 100 to 250 in attendance, show the most decline.

Willow Creek's Self-Evaluation

In North America, the megachurch movement is largely a Boomer-generated phenomenon. The cultural impact of that generation is on the wane, however, as it gives way to Generation X and Generation Y, which represent different approaches to spirituality and a more relational self-awareness. Church leaders recognize that their congregations are aging and that their attempts to retain those in the years of "delayed adulthood" have not been as effective as they had hoped.[8] Simply making the style of worship more culturally appropriate and the atmosphere more intimate, while waiting for young adults to mature and be ready to participate in "real church," has not worked.

These younger generations are looking for a different kind of church that is less program-oriented and event-focused, and more relational, empowering, incarnational, and community engaged. They challenge the attractional model of ministry as being the last hurrah of modernity, a throwback to the Christendom mentality. Even the cultural phenomenon of delayed adulthood is being challenged by the resurgent Reformed movement that is thriving among young people and calling them to a countercultural approach to spirituality.[9]

The leadership of Willow Creek Community Church is aware of the cultural transition that is underway. In response, it embarked upon a three-year self-assessment, the results of which were published in 2007 as *Reveal: Where Are You?*[10] They tested three hypotheses to explore to what extent people's involvement in the church was connected to their spiritual growth in Christ:

Hypothesis 1: There is a migration path for spiritual growth based on church activities.

Hypothesis 2: The most effective evangelism tool is a spiritual conversation.

Hypothesis 3: Spiritual relationships are a key driver of spiritual growth.[11]

In order to obtain reliable data, Willow Creek conducted extensive field research in 2004, analyzing 6,000 attendee surveys, plus 300 surveys completed by people who had left Willow Creek within the previous year. In 2007 5,000 surveys were completed by congregants of Willow Creek and six other churches across the United States. Though the church sample was quite small, the researchers argued that it covered both independent and denominational churches and was representative of geographic, age, and cultural diversity. More-over, at the beginning and end of the process (in 2004 and 2007), Willow Creek conducted an additional 120 one-on-one conversations that explored in depth the spiritual lives of the participants.[12]

The Findings of Reveal

Whereas many critics accuse megachurches of being mainly pre-occupied with numbers, *Reveal* demonstrates Bill Hybels' concern for the spiritual comprehension and growth of the Willow Creek congregation, and the extraordinary lengths to which the church's leadership was prepared to go to obtain an accurate assessment of that. On the bright side, the research revealed that fifty percent of the congregation "loved God more than anything else and were reaching out to their unchurched friends and serving the poor on a regular basis."[13] On this issue, the survey could have been more specific in order to ascertain people's depth of theological and doctrinal under-standing. What particularly disturbed Bill Hybels, though, was the fact that "nearly one out of every four people at Willow Creek was stalled in their spiritual growth or dissatisfied with the church—and many of them were considering leaving."[14]

The numbered paragraphs that follow represent the principal findings of the *Reveal* report, followed by my own comments made from a missional perspective and with the post-Boomer generations especially in mind.

1. Involvement in church activities does not predict or drive long-term spiritual growth. But there is a "spiritual continuum" that is very predictive and powerful. People who were more involved in church activities did not express a greater love for God than people who were less involved. In other words, an increasing level of involvement in activities does not *predict* an increasing love for God.[15] But they are more likely to serve, tithe, etc. There was strong evidence of a spiritual continuum:

Exploring Christianity → Growing in Christ → Close to Christ → Christ Centered

Comment: I assume that a programmatic approach to spiritual formation does not give sufficient regard to the fact that individuals are at different starting points, have to deal with different issues if they are to make spiritual progress, have different learning styles, and move at a different pace. What is appropriate for a school curriculum may not be appropriate for discipleship training. There is no evidence that Jesus used such a sequential and programmatic learning model in the training of his disciples! His method represented situational learning, combining observation, reflection, and working under supervision. The disciples learned through being in daily contact with their mentor.

2. Spiritual growth is all about increasing relational closeness to Christ. But the dilemma pointed out in the report is: "If the activities of the church are all about turning people toward Christ and encouraging them to grow spiritually, why doesn't there appear to be a solid connection between participation in church activities and spiritual growth?"[16]

Comment: This principle relates to my reflections on the first finding. "Relational closeness" does not spontaneously come about in a classroom or seminar context, which leads to a further consideration: namely, why does the typical suburban small group not establish a *spiritual* relational closeness to Christ when the home-atmosphere setting is conducive to fostering a corresponding *social* relational closeness? Those small groups that best facilitate both kinds of relational closeness to Christ are most likely to consist of individuals whose lives intersect during the week outside of church-related activities, and in which a high level of trust has developed, allowing members to let down their guards and remove their masks. Unfortunately, with many suburban small groups the same degree of disconnect from their wider social context is as evident in their group as it is in the worship service and centralized program gatherings, and they do little to foster relational closeness.[17] Although the group members are meeting in decentralized locations, they continue to perpetuate an inwardly focused mentality.

3. *The church is most important in the early stages of spiritual growth.* Its role then shifts from being the primary influence to being a secondary influence. The church does not drive long-term spiritual growth. Spiritual practices, such as prayer, journaling, solitude, and studying Scripture, play an increasingly important role over time as individuals seek to grow in their relationship with Christ.[18]

Comment: Here we see the influence of our Western culture of individualism, and an attendant privatization of faith, both of which stem from modernity. Every church, whatever its size, faces this challenge. Our faith in Christ only grows through the fostering of a *personal* relationship, which is not the same as a *private* relationship. Individualism and privatization of faith are not simply neutral social constructs, but are antithetical to a biblical understanding of fellowship, hospitality, and corporate service.

The people of God (*ekklesia*) are called out from the world to experience a new quality of relationship that is made possible by a common allegiance to Christ, a living-out of the gospel through the indwelling of the Holy Spirit. Communities of believers are charged with the mission of proclaiming Christ in the world. Such is the complex nature of fellowship (*koinonia*) that defines our understanding of "church." Because of the range of its activities, as well as the complexity of human relationships, a megachurch faces the challenge of expressing authentic *koinonia* to an even greater degree than the smaller church.

In all fairness it must be recognized that many smaller churches assume they experience "true" community when, in reality, they are quite dysfunctional and exclusionary. Bill Donahue comments that smallness can foster a "small town" mentality that is very much "outsider *un*friendly." He observes that the two larger churches in which he has served, in contrast to a small congregation of

120, were less intimidating, friendlier, and more open. He rightly says that the issue is quality of relationships and adherence to the gospel.[19]

To the extent that church members, as they mature, find the church to be less important to them than their relationship with Christ, so questions surface about the very nature of the church. As Christians mature in their faith, we should expect their love for the church to deepen rather than diminish. When this expectation is not realized, churches need to examine with candor and humility why Christians become jaded and decide to leave.[20] Again, this concern is by no means restricted to megachurches, but extends to so many churches that have been impacted by modernity.

4. *Personal spiritual practices are the building blocks for a Christ-centered life.* "The research strongly suggests that the church declines in influence as people grow spiritually." The conclusion based on the data is this: The church doesn't need to hold the hands of people who are moving through the later stages of the spiritual continuum. An authentic Christ-centered life is fundamentally the result of a strong commitment to a growing *personal relationship* with Jesus Christ.[21]

Comment: This reflects the outworking of consumerist and individualistic assumptions that lie at the heart of so many churches in the West, and not just the seeker-sensitive model of megachurch. Every church's influence declines as the congregation becomes inwardly focused. The worship experience of many individuals is nonrelational because of their privatized worship disposition, whatever the size of the church, and especially when their involvement does not extend beyond attendance at a worship service. Beyond that, personal contacts made through seminars and classes tend to be shallow, because people's lives seldom, if ever, intersect outside of these gatherings.

The majority of churches located in suburban settings, as well as those in urban locations characterized by high population turnover, find that people's daily lives are fragmented by a diversity of disconnected activities and social networks. Such social disconnect means that the church struggles to demonstrate any kind of communal expression of faith. Apart from churches, most other institutions struggle to maintain the loyalty and cohesion of their members because of the same cultural challenges.

Churches under the prevailing assumptions and influence of Christendom are highly structured for *gathering* but not for *dispersing*. To the extent that they are not rooted in local communities, neighborhoods, and networks of relationships, they thereby become disconnected and remote. Churches function as places to which people have to be invited, rather than as faith communities that intersect with the wider community on many issues and provide multiple entry points.

5. *A church's most active evangelists, volunteers, and donors come from the most spiritually advanced segments.* This finding came as a surprise. "We had long operated under the assumption that evangelism fervor is at its highest early on in a person's faith journey. This was based on the thinking that newer believers had more passion for their faith, as well as long-standing relationships with others who had not yet given their lives to Christ. Also, serving is often seen as an early door opener in the faith journey. These results caused us to reevaluate deeply rooted beliefs."[22]

Comment: Would these findings hold true for persons who have undergone a deep-level, life-changing conversion experience, and for whom "church" represents a community of believers that knew them and of newfound friends who surrounded them with their love? When community service is largely expressed as programs run by the church, then new people have to first be socialized into the church before they are likely to get involved. However, when Christians working together in a neighborhood draw attention to needs, whether local or global, it is much easier to invite others to become involved. There are many stories of individuals who were not believers at the time of their initial involvement coming to faith as a result of working alongside neighbors and friends, motivated by the love of Christ to respond to human need. It is a case of belonging before believing. At the same time, it must be emphasized that belonging in the deeper sense of *identity*, as distinct from *association*, doesn't happen without belief. The two go hand in hand.

6. *More than 25 percent of those surveyed described themselves as spiritually "stalled" or "dissatisfied" with the role of the church in their*

spiritual growth.[23] The stalled segment reports much lower levels of spiritual practices than other believer segments. "25 percent—one out of four—are considering leaving the church."[24] As we have previously noted, just over half of those surveyed participate in small groups that meet once a month or more, but to what extent do the members of these groups interact with each other in the course of daily life? How well do they really get to know each other? The report observes that there is clearly a lack of spiritual mentoring, with just 4 percent of the dissatisfied segment (noted above) and 25 percent of all who were surveyed reporting being satisfied with the church's help in providing a spiritual mentor.[25]

Comment: The people who self-identified in this category acknowledged the existence of significant barriers to spiritual growth, including addictions, inappropriate relationships, emotional issues, and not prioritizing one's spiritual life. Their sense of being stalled or dissatisfied may also reflect another sort of addiction that is evident in our culture: namely, an adrenaline addiction that lessens our ability to appreciate the "dull routines" of daily discipleship and instead produces emotional "highs" that in turn stimulate the need for yet more intense experiences. Much of life, however, consists of "the same old thing," which tests our patience, humility, and faithfulness. Willow Creek is to be commended for building a small group structure that enabled them to identify these people. So many churches lack the basic building blocks of relational communities in which trust levels could be developed and mutual accountability, intercession, and encouragement fostered. The barriers to spiritual growth may reflect a general desire for "therapeutic" and "technique"-dependent approaches, instead of the recognition that in the Christian life we should expect suffering and difficulties. Some problems do indeed have solutions, while others are simply facts of life that we have to learn to live with.

The *Reveal* study recognizes, "The dissatisfied segment has people who are some of the most involved in the church and who are trying to grow in their faith. However, the research shows they are also the ones most likely to report that they are considering leaving the church."[26] Could their attitude reflect a growing sense of disconnect between the issues they face and the way the church is programmed to address their perceived needs? Alternatively, it may indicate the heavy demand that a high-performance and highly programmatic approach to ministry places on a shrinking pool of suitably qualified and available volunteers. They may contemplate leaving to avoid burnout.

It is their sense of loyalty to a church that has meant so much to them and their ongoing commitment to Christ and the advance of the gospel that keeps them in place. The high percentage of dissatisfied persons (10 percent) indicates that there may be systemic issues that need to be addressed as a matter of urgency. Willow Creek, as a result of its survey, comments, "Much like parents, the church may need to shift its relationship with its maturing disciples into something different in order to maintain an appropriate level of influence and provide the support they need."[27]

Responding to the Findings of the Reveal Report

The *Reveal* report moves beyond analysis and the need for further study to take the next steps in implementation.

. *1. Our message to the congregation has to change.* "We want to move people from dependence on the church to a growing interdependent partnership with the church."[28]

Comment: While people need to learn how to feed themselves through personal spiritual practices that allow them to deepen their relationship with Christ, this individualistic emphasis needs to go hand in hand with membership in a local expression of the body of Christ that is involved with the broader community on a daily basis.[29] Willow Creek has an impressive record of engaging in a wide range of ministries, both locally and globally. The challenge they face is how to engage those who have become either overly dependent, on the one hand, or increasingly independent, on the other. Once again this issue is not confined to megachurches. The strength of the "household" churches of the New Testament lay in the fact that they represented a basic economic building block of society, as well as a domestic unit. Believers lived out their Christian faith in company with others alongside whom they lived and worked.

David Fitch, a pastor and professor in Illinois, identifies an embedded consumerist approach in the *Reveal* report's response to the challenges of spiritual growth. Personal needs are to be met and serviced by the church. However, according to Fitch, spiritual growth cannot be facilitated simply on an individual basis "separate from community." He draws attention to the interpersonal emphasis of spiritual growth in the New Testament letters to the churches: "confessing sin one to another (James 5:16), speaking truth as real people to other people we know in love (Eph. 4:25), . . . working out our lives in regular communal fellowship in submission one to another (Phil. 2:1–12) . . . These practices cannot be mass-organized. They take intentional community."[30]

This message of interdependence runs contrary to an individualistic culture of self-reliance. But there is increasing evidence that our self-focused, consumerist society will be unsustainable in the long run. People will need to lead more integrated lives through the building of communities with housing available for various income levels, so that people at every stage of life can be in contact with one another. Employment, shopping, and health and recreational facilities will need to be within easy reach and served by frequent and efficient local, public transportation. This is the vision of the "new urbanism."[31]

Architects are developing new townships and working for urban renewal with these considerations in mind. Rather than perpetuating interminable urban sprawl, creating suburban development with few amenities and with housing designed for a homogeneous population segment, we need places where people of all ages and income levels can put down roots and gain a sense of belonging. If we fail to take these strategic planning initiatives, we will face a future of increasing traffic logjams, escalating crime rates, depression, and domestic violence. Churches have a key role to play and a prophetic voice that needs to be heard in the context of new urbanism.

2. We need to coach next steps. "We want to transition the role of the church from spiritual parent to spiritual coach."[32]

Comment: Here is the frank admission that there is no one-size-fits-all spiritual growth plan.[33] Spiritual coaching must not be confined to an individualistic, customized "workout" model. Instead the small groups themselves provide a context for peer coaching, recognizing that the value of any such coaching is only as good as the peers providing it. Spiritual fitness must be worked out in the context of community, in which the various members of the body of Christ provide their contribution to the well-being of the whole. The body does not consist of one member but of many, with each individual part contributing to the whole according to its location and function (1 Cor. 12:12–27). Mentoring should include both individual and peer mentoring, with persons gifted and trained to fulfill those roles. We learn together as we grow together, enriched by each other's struggles, insights, and experiences. It is imperative that each faith community be about mission as an antidote to becoming ingrown. This challenge is not confined to megachurches but is pervasive among churches of all sizes.

3. *We need to extend the impact of our weekend services.* Willow Creek sees the need to extend the impact of their weekend service to meet the needs of those who are farther along in the journey. For instance, for their five-week series on James, they distributed a journal with space for taking notes (Exploring), questions for individuals to use throughout the week (Growing in Christ), and questions for use in small groups (Growing) or with a spiritual friend (Close to Christ). They also included insights from biblical commentary for those who wanted to dig deeper (Christ-Centered). The initial response has been very positive.

Comment: This approach still represents a programmatic response, raising the question as to how effective it will prove in the long run in addressing the needs of such a diverse crowd of individuals. It is commendable to have a range of resources at hand, but the church's effectiveness in addressing the challenges it has identified will also depend on the quality of the relationships that are developed and the building of local faith communities that represent a holistic spirituality applied to every area of life.

Willow Creek Community Church is to be commended for both the thoroughness and the professionalism of its research and, even more so, that it has made the results public. Many churches with such a high public profile would have kept the results under wraps and restricted access to their own leadership, even keeping the members in the dark. But Willow Creek has published its results for the benefit of other churches. There are important lessons to be learned not only for other megachurches and for the churches in the Willow Creek Association, but also for churches of all sizes and traditions. The report admits that it is only scratching the surface; much more investigation, analysis, and interpretation of the results need to be undertaken.

Further Examples

This chapter has devoted a disproportionate amount of space to Willow Creek because of its high international profile and the in-depth nature of its self-study. It is not, however, offered as a case study of a typical megachurch, for they come in different types and sizes. Scott Thumma in fact identifies four different types: old-line, program-based; seeker; charismatic, pastor-focused; and new-wave, re-envisioned churches.[34] Peter Brierley, a veteran researcher of churches in the United Kingdom, believes that the myths attached to megachurches in the United States are almost identically true of those in the United Kingdom, bearing in mind that a church of four hundred in the United Kingdom is essentially the equivalent of a two thousand–member megachurch in the United States.[35]

Among a number of megachurch leaders, the realization is growing that in order to be truly missional, their churches must adopt a more decentralized approach. The era of Christendom is fast fading, and with it, the declining effectiveness of attractional strategies. The church's message must change from, "Come to us in order to learn what the gospel of the reign of God is all about" to, "We will come to you to live among you in order to discover how the good news can impact all of our lives."

• Christian Assembly (Calgary, Alberta) •

With Willow Creek having taken the lead in recognizing the value of the "if you won't come to us, we'll come to you" approach, other churches in the Willow Creek Association and beyond are poised to follow. For instance, Christian Assembly Calgary, the largest evangelical church in Canada, is moving in a similar direction—that is, becoming more missional by decentralizing and developing neighborhood-based faith communities. This is a significant change in emphasis considering that Calgary is the fastest growing city in the nation, with an abundance of empty space for suburban development on a grand scale.

• Community of Joy (Glendale, Arizona) •

I was first made aware of this change in emphasis when Walt Kallestad of Community Church of Joy, in Glendale, Arizona, began to seriously question his long held and successfully implemented consumer church assumptions. For the past twenty years he had built up a seeker-friendly Evangelical Lutheran Church of America (ELCA) congregation to become one of the largest churches in his denomination, with a membership of twelve thousand. Despite the numerical success, he had come to see that "his huge flock had lost its community, its authenticity—its passion."[36] Walt had this to say about his initial moment of realization:

> After my heart attack and six-way bypass in January 2002, I began to consider who might be the successor to my ministry. It would have to be just the right person, someone capable of raising and managing a multi-million dollar budget as well as the staff and programs of a megachurch. It would need to be someone who could effectively reach the twenty- and thirty-year-olds I was struggling to reach.
>
> I discussed this idea with other pastors across the country. But it was in Washington, DC that I felt the ground shaking all around me. "Why would anyone want your church?" a pastor there responded. "Anyone who is serious about ministry today does not want to be stuck raising money for maintaining buildings and mortgages. They want to be on the cutting edge making a difference." As hard as it was to hear, I knew what he had just said was right.[37]

After recovering from his bypass surgery, Walt took a sabbatical, his first in twenty-seven years, during which time he visited Mike Breen, the pastor and then team leader of St. Thomas' Church (an Anglican and Baptist church) in Sheffield, England. This contact led to a continuing friendship in which was birthed the realization that Community Church of Joy had to focus on making authentic Christ followers who could then form clusters to live out their faith and reach out into their neighborhoods.[38]

• Wooddale Church (Eden Prairie, Minnesota) •

Wooddale Church is located in the southwest suburbs of the Twin Cities, an area with a higher percentage of church-attending people than most other metropolitan areas. Leith Anderson pastors this congregation, which has a history of more than fifty years. Unlike many older churches it has sustained healthy growth over the years, with significant conversion growth. Daniel Collison, the church's worship pastor, attributes Wooddale's health to the fact that "God has provided extraordinary blessings on the work of Wooddale Church. There is no other reasonable explanation for the amount of new conversions, the ability to successfully start and assist new churches, outreach capacity that impacts local and global communities, numeric growth, and continually healthy financials."[39] This is a church with a clear sense of direction and strong commitment to core values expressed in their purpose statement and covenant.

Purpose Statement: The purpose of Wooddale Church is to honor God by making more disciples for Jesus Christ.

Covenant: A disciple commits to obey Jesus Christ as Savior and Lord in knowledge of God, service for God and sharing of God. Based upon this purpose, we do covenant together by God's grace, to live our lives consistent with the standards of biblical teaching; including the support of this local ministry in attendance, prayer, service and giving, by living lives in word and deed that are an encouragement to others to know and be like Jesus Christ, and by reflecting in all our relationships the servant-love of our Lord.[40]

Like most churches in the Western world, small as well as large, Wooddale works hard to counteract the culture of consumerism, with its lack of commitment and shop-around mentality. It struggles with a widening gap between weekly attendance and church membership, with 13,000-plus members but an average weekly attendance of only 4,700—which no doubt reflects the reality that churchgoers are less frequent in their attendance than in former years. The general pattern across traditions, regardless of the size of the church, is that only between 30 and 40 percent of members are in church on any given Sunday. This applies to the United Kingdom as much as to North America.

It is encouraging to encounter megachurches committed to church planting. The method adopted by Wooddale is to begin new churches by a "large baby birth process." "Wooddale invites hundreds of its constituents to leave Wooddale for the purpose of investing their time and resources in new church starts. Often times, the new church starts begin with multiple staff and worship services on the first weekend of public worship services."[41] Collison compares this method to the act of donating blood.

• Megachurches in the United Kingdom •

It was long assumed that megachurches were much less likely to occur in the United Kingdom than in the United States. This conclusion was based on the following considerations: cities in the United Kingdom are more compact and congested; parking is severely limited; public transportation is reduced on Sundays; and the population is generally less mobile than in the United States. In recent years, however, a number of churches with congregations numbering in the thousands have defied this assumption. For instance, Kingsway International Christian Centre in Hackney, London, regularly draws 12,000-plus on a Sunday; Ruach Ministries Christian Centre, also in London, 4,200; and Redeemed Church of God in Brent, 2,500, as part of a denomination of some 133 congregations. And Hillsong Church in London, a megachurch movement birthed in Australia, draws 6,000 and has just started a new church in Sheffield with 1,000 currently attending.[42]

Vulnerability of Megachurches

The megachurch phenomenon has come of age to the extent that it engages in critical self-reflection, in relation to both the lessons learned from its past experience and the challenges posed by the traumatic cultural transitions that are taking place. We identified five of these megatrends in our opening chapter. Every church, regardless of its size, ecclesiastical tradition, or location, is impacted sooner or later by these changes, but in some respects megachurches are especially vulnerable. Some of the concerns that surface most regularly in the course of conversation with their leaders are discussed in what follows.

The first concern that is most evident, particularly among those megachurches that have been in existence for twenty years or more, is the increasing average age of the congregation. This is especially true for churches in communities that have ceased to expand, and that no longer attract young families.[43] It becomes even more evident when the ethnic composition of the surrounding community undergoes radical change and the church struggles in its attempt to connect with this new population. An aging leadership also contributes to the aging of the population. Once again, this aging phenomenon is not confined to megachurches, but is a challenge facing most churches that are more than twenty to thirty years old.

The aging process is becoming increasingly evident in churches that attracted a predominantly Boomer congregation in the 1980s, when many were raising families. But, as we noted above, many of the children of Boomers have left the churches of their youth in search of a different expression of church than the one their parents preferred. As long as the areas served by these megachurches attract primarily Boomers, they will continue to maintain their numbers, but their membership will continually increase in its average age.

Furthermore, we must not overlook the increasing prevalence of second marriages among Boomers, which often results in the starting of a second family. Boomers will continue to exert a significant influence due to their numerical strength, economic resources, and increased life expectancy. But they must be careful not to sacrifice the future by alienating subsequent generations by holding on too tightly to the traditions they cherished, in the same way that the Builder generation alienated them!

The second concern relates to worries about a possible serious downturn in the national economy and the increasing vulnerability of

Western nations to global power plays over things like oil and cheaper manufacturing and technical advances overseas. How competitive can developed countries remain in world markets? Megachurches are especially vulnerable because they represent multimillion-dollar operations. Their extensive facilities, high-tech equipment, large program budgets, and administrative staffs mean high running expenses and a large payroll. They pay top rates for their senior staff, due to the small size of the pool of sufficiently qualified people and the competition among megachurches drawing from that small pool. They also recruit from the professional world, among committed Christians who are prepared to take a significant pay cut yet whose pay scales remain much higher than the average church worker.

The huge budgets of megachurches are heavily reliant on a small percentage of individuals with the financial resources and commitment to make generous contributions. In many churches, the 80/20 percent rule applies: twenty percent of the congregation provides eighty percent of the finances. For megachurches, the percentage of the congregation that is able to provide significant financial support is even smaller. Consequently, any serious economic downturn that impacts investment income and performance bonuses will have serious repercussions for the church, leading to staff layoffs and mortgage repayment difficulties. Unlike many long-established churches, most megachurches do not have endowments provided by previous generations to draw upon.

A further complication is that megachurches attract their congregation from a large catchment area, which has led to the perennial problem of figuring out how to involve attendees beyond their weekly worship experience when many of the attendees live more than thirty miles, or a twenty-minute driving time, away. This concern initiated the need for a more decentralized approach. Increasing urgency has been introduced to the discussion by the steep rise in gas prices, coupled with higher living costs brought about by the sub-prime mortgage crisis. An increasing number of families have to find ways to cut their budgets, and reducing fuel costs represents one cost-saving measure. But it is a measure that is not without ramifications in terms of their involvement with the church.

The possibility of churches losing their tax-exempt status represents another, albeit more remote, issue. There have been rumblings of this in some government circles, with a number of megachurch ministries coming under the scrutiny of the Internal Revenue Service in the United States, especially those with high-profile television ministries led by pastors indulging in lavish lifestyles.

Pastors who fail to handle the pressures of ministry appropriately and promptly are in danger of experiencing eventual burnout, drug and alcohol abuse, and moral failure. The larger the church, the greater the pressures become. When church leaders fall, the consequences for the congregation are devastating. In the case of the moral lapse of a megachurch pastor the repercussions are even more serious than when it occurs in smaller churches. For the wider Christian community, the news attracts national media attention, bringing a sense of betrayal. For the church members, it is catastrophic, because their high-profile church has engendered high expectations. Once these hopes have been dashed, significant numbers stop attending, either to go elsewhere or to disassociate entirely from institutional religion.

Summary

Just as the megachurch movement pioneered the high-profile, seeker-attracting model of the 1980s, some megachurches are now poised to make a strategic contribution in the developing of missional strategies in the twenty-first century. They need to work in tandem with more than three hundred thousand much smaller churches, many of which are far more rooted in neighborhoods, many with a long history of association with their neighborhoods.[44] To the extent that they enter into a genuinely reciprocal partnership, they will no longer be perceived as a threat, but as providing mutually beneficial resources as training centers and rallying points for Christian celebration.

As the morphing of the church takes place through churches of all sizes identified either with the missional church or emerging church conversations, those churches that persist in maintaining a come-to-us, Christendom mentality will be challenged and inspired to shift from a survival to a missional mode. Or, where they are experiencing success in attracting a crowd, the challenge will be to shift from an attitude of triumphalism to one of humble engagement, working toward the transformation of their communities. The current expansion of megachurches should not lead them to a sense of false security. In the long term, they will not be immune to the downturn looming over denominations in general and will have to face the consequences of the demise of struggling, smaller churches that have unwittingly served as their feeder system.

__5__ ── ── ─

urban engagement

Large numbers of white Anglo-Saxon Protestant (WASP) churches have fled the city for the suburbs. The strongest churches in urban contexts are Roman Catholic, African-American, Pentecostal, Salvation Army, and in particular the churches established by recent immigrants from Asia, Latin America, and Africa. It must also be said that traditional denominations, with a parish mentality inherited from their European history, have struggled valiantly to maintain a presence despite the shifting demographics. They have demonstrated more resilience than churches that lack this sense of close identity with their neighborhoods. A number of these traditional denominational churches have transitioned into congregations that are no longer predominantly white, with indigenous leadership. Such churches often represent the growing edge of traditional churches in older, transitional urban locations.

Any urban engagement must take into account the diversity of cultures and networks that are represented in the surrounding community. It is easy to become overwhelmed by the sheer size and complexity of the city. Each city is unique, and every district has its distinctive characteristics. The city as a whole must be understood in terms of its history, its industry and economy, its changing demographics, and the social issues that confront it. Engagement in urban mission entails immersion in the popular culture that is so pervasive. This is what is required in endeavoring to exegete the city.

At the ground level, ministry needs to be based on a block-by-block approach. A number of North American churches have initiated an "adopt-a-block strategy," in which they pray for individuals, develop relationships, and help them in practical ways, such as painting a fence, shoveling snow, babysitting their children, and taking food over when sickness strikes.[1] Such a strategy must be an expression of genuine love for the other person, with no strings attached.

Examples of Urban Engagement

In contrast to the many examples of church closures and congregations that struggle to maintain their day-to-day existence, there are also stories of urban churches that encourage and inspire. None of the churches mentioned in this chapter hold themselves up as models to be emulated, because they recognize their own limitations and continue to live on a steep learning curve. But I am grateful that some of those mentioned have given permission for their stories to be told, while others have made their stories available through their Web sites. What follows is only a small sampling of the churches that are actively engaging in ministry in their urban contexts; many more could certainly be cited, were it not for the limitations of space and my own knowledge.

• Emmanuel Reformed Church (Paramount, California) •

Emmanuel Reformed Church is a church whose very existence comes as a surprise, considering its origins and the radical changes that its surrounding community has undergone over the years. Dutch dairy farmers founded the church in the 1920s in what was then a self-contained farming community to the south of Los Angeles. Worship services were originally held in Dutch, but in the 1940s they made the switch to English, which broadened their ministry vision to include all varieties of people.[2]

As time went by, the city of Paramount underwent a radical transformation. It was no longer a community of dairy farmers but was absorbed into the Los Angeles sprawl. It became a low-income area populated by Latinos, blacks, a sprinkling of Asians, and a rapidly diminishing white population. Housing deteriorated, businesses were suffering, and the city struggled to maintain educational, police, and other social services. By 1980 Paramount was pronounced by the Rand Corporation as the fourth worst small city in America. The people of Emmanuel Reformed Church could have followed the so-called white flight of other traditional denominations, but instead decided to remain where they were. The Reverend Harold Korver has provided visionary leadership since 1970, with his constant refrain being, "through tradition into mission." Harold's son Ken—who grew up in Paramount and now serves as the senior pastor—used to set off for school each day with his father's reminder that he was a missionary.

Against all odds, the church has continued to grow, now with five worship services that reflect the ethnic mix of the neighborhood. Bill White, the outreach pastor, writes, "We're an odd mix of people—a melting pot of cultures, ages, socio-economic classes, religious backgrounds and races. By many standards, we shouldn't even exist, and we certainly shouldn't be growing. And yet, here we are, thriving in our urban Los Angeles community and unashamedly committed to transform not only our neighborhood but our world."[3] The transition that the church has helped bring about has been far from easy. The leadership has exercised much patience and understanding in helping its members, especially those who have been around since the earliest days, weather the changes.

Emmanuel Reformed Church belongs to a historic denomination, to which it has remained loyal over the years. Its pastor has been president of the denomination and a leader in theological education. The church has trained over fifty interns to become Reformed Church pastors. This church could just as well have been included in the previous chapter, but I decided that its more defining significance lay in its impressive commitment to urban mission and as an agent of change within the denomination. They describe themselves as an emerging missional church.

Alan Roxburgh and Fred Romanuk define a missional church as "a community of God's people who live into the imagination that they are, by their very nature, God's missionary people living as a demonstration of what God plans to do in and for all of creation in Jesus Christ."[4] Bill White speaks for the leadership team of the church when he confesses that "mission is both who we are and who we hope to be."[5] Their intention is crystallized in their vision statement, "Emmanuel Church: deeply connecting people to Jesus, people, and mission."[6]

Emmanuel Reformed Church is there for the long haul. They are not simply concerned to grow but to work for the transformation of the city of Paramount. They have taken their inspiration from Isaiah's prophecy: "The Spirit of the Sovereign Lord is on me, because the Lord has anointed me to preach good news to the poor. He has sent me to bind up the brokenhearted, to proclaim freedom for the captives and release from darkness for the prisoners, to proclaim the year of the Lord's favor . . ." (Isa. 61:1–2). They have seen this vision become a reality to a remarkable degree. Here is Bill White's summary:

> We've worked closely with the city and served in whatever way we could. A handful of Emmanuelites have served as mayor and city councilors in the past few decades. Our "Looking Good" program of painting houses took off—we painted over 400 houses in Paramount. We coached the teams in our local schools. We did whatever we could do. Recently, Paramount received the "All American City" award because of our huge strides in fighting crime, building community pride, creating jobs, and flourishing public works—and the City Manager, who is not a churchgoer, spoke to our congregation and frankly said that Emmanuel was the spark that catalyzed the change.[7]

Yet, while celebrating significant progress, it is readily admitted that much remains to be done, especially in the school system, which still has the poorest performance records in the state of California.

The church has now turned its attention to the neighboring city of Compton—a vision that was brought before the congregation in a sermon by the head pastor, in which he described how God was calling Emmanuel Church to commit the next forty years to the redevelopment of the city of Compton, a predominantly African-American area of Los Angeles, in partnership with the churches in the city. In a video clip during that sermon, pastor Ken Korver stood with their African-American pastor Larry Dove in the Los Angeles riverbed (it's dry for most of the year!), which separates Paramount from Compton, and pointed toward Compton. At about that same time the national news media published that Compton ranked as the fourth worst US city to live in—the same ranking that Paramount had received a number of years previously. Pastor Ken Korver later met with the mayor of Compton, a meeting that developed into a relationship of friendship and trust. As a result Ken has been invited to speak to the city council, the Compton school board, and at the Compton community leadership breakfast.

There is increasing recognition that the churches in economically deprived and socially troubled neighborhoods play a key role in addressing the challenges faced by the community. Once again, Emmanuel Reformed Church is beginning by beautifying the neighborhood. The postmaster of Compton has helped identify the houses that would most benefit from a face-lift, or in some cases an even more radical makeover, through information provided by the mail deliverers, who know their areas intimately as they cover the ground on a daily basis. Local churches are joining in a cleanup campaign, with their numbers swelled by help from other churches, including Saddleback Community Church in affluent Orange County. Local businesses, including the health care organization Kaiser Permanente, are also getting involved.

Sporting amenities also play a significant role in the rejuvenation of a city committed to urban renewal. Mindful of the Latino population's love of soccer, members of Emmanuel are sponsoring not only Compton's first recreation league, but its first competitive league as well. Plans are on the table for a multimillion dollar, state-of-the-art soccer training facility. The church's Web site displays a picture of Ivan Velasquez, one of their future church planters, sitting on a bench in Compton. The backrest of the bench is made up of a set of tiles painted by one of their Compton leaders, portraying their vision of how the city will look one day. A vision must be translated into community commitment and public declaration of that commitment.

If the intentions outlined above are to represent authentic signs of the kingdom in the city, the church must walk in humility, giving all the glory to God. Bill White underlines this point when he says,

> Perhaps the single biggest key to the development of the partnerships has been Ken's insistence that Emmanuel receive no recognition for its efforts in Compton. . . . We heard from friends who live in Compton that those same leaders moved from being endeared to actually believing Ken when the *Compton Courier* newspaper came out with a front page article about the Compton work days and it simply referenced "a church in a nearby city" as the catalyst (because Ken would not let them mention Emmanuel's name). This is the sort of attitude that's been crucial for our credibility in Compton, and it has helped with our partners on the outside as well.[8]

While the church welcomes the contribution of Christians from outside, it is strongly committed to raising up indigenous leadership through mentoring. Their head pastor recently had everyone in the leadership team submit a list of the individuals they had been in touch with in the relational aspect of their ministry. Each person made three lists of the concentric circles of their impact: those they were discipling, those they were investing in, and those they were influencing. Out of these relationships will emerge the next generation of leadership, not only for the Paramount church, but also for the new initiatives in neighboring Compton. They are committed to in-ministry formation and not just for-ministry preparation. They recognize that as much learning takes place on the streets as in the classroom, if not more.

We conclude our consideration of Emmanuel Reformed Church with Bill White's recounting, after a Thanksgiving service, of the testimonies of a number of individuals who have become part of the Compton initiative:

> We had a dozen prison inmates come up on stage and share their stories of meeting Jesus in our recovery ministry in their facility and

on Sundays here on their weekly passes. A guy who graduated from that prison ministry earlier this year shared how he's now leading a bible study for a hundred students at the local community college. Then our janitor shared about his transformation from living on the streets to being employed at the church and becoming a good friend to the head pastor. Then a recent convert shared his story of going through Alpha this fall and transitioning from agnostic to believer. Then an ex-gangbanger from Compton shared about why he's a part of Emmanuel—because of our outreach in Compton. Finally a couple shared their story about how turned off they were when their new neighbors moved in. "We thought they were foster parents," Alma said, "because there was every color of person helping them move in. Then we found out they were church people, and that was even worse!" They then shared about how they met Jesus through their neighbors, got to serve in what was once rival gang territory in Compton, and now worship in that same "foster parent" house church next door.[9]

This is a church with much to celebrate, but which readily admits that it has much to learn. In the words of senior pastor Ken Korver: "What we are all about is prayerfully and humbly trying to actually become followers of Jesus Christ." Its commitment to such a challenging long-term project as the one in Compton will keep it on a steep learning curve in the coming days and years.

• Canadian Examples •

Cam Roxburgh, who has his finger on the pulse of developments in Canada, points to the example of Ed Topp in Calgary, who gets his people to serve in the local neighborhood one Sunday a month. Instead of "Sunday service," it becomes "Service Sunday." Joyce Rees (formerly Heron) leads a community of people in the downtown east side of Vancouver who are working to bring about significant social and economic improvements. Tim Dichau leads a church, also in Vancouver, called Grandview Calvary that is attempting to live out a vision "to extend the radical welcome of God in Christ for the transformation" of their local neighborhood.[10] These few snapshots can hardly do justice to the many forms of urban engagement that are taking place in the churches of Canada, but they are nonetheless harbingers, I believe, of what is to come for churches south of the border.

• The Eden Project (Manchester, England) •

Manchester, England, is located at the heart of where the Industrial Revolution was birthed in Britain beginning in the first part of the nineteenth century. The development of new industries and the building of factories at that time triggered a large-scale urban migration. The churches, however, were slow to recognize the extent of this social phenomenon and to appreciate its economic and cultural repercussions. Belatedly, a spate of church and chapel construction began in the 1830s, which received fresh momentum in the 1860s and 1870s, but by then it was a case of too little too late. In the industrial heartland it was not that the churches lost the working classes; rather, it never had them in the first place.

The missionary challenge presented by the old industrial centers of Britain remains to this day. The church has struggled to survive in many of the decaying areas of the inner city, where the centers of manufacture have moved to areas of the world where labor is cheaper and more plentiful. Abandoned and derelict factories blight the landscape, until they can be demolished and replaced by new commercial estates, shopping malls, and housing developments. Until then, they remain centers of high crime, family breakdown, youth unemployment, drug dealing, and decaying public housing.

The first Eden Partnership began in 1997 in one of the worst areas of Manchester, Wythenshawe, a district that derives its name from an old English word meaning "willow wood."[11] Today it is Manchester's largest district, consisting of a massive housing estate where an overspill population could be housed from the slum squalor of the central wards.[12]

> The upheaval and resettlement of such large numbers of people took little account of social evolution or community spirit, neither of which existed, so that by the late 20th century Wythenshawe suffered many social problems. First, the estate was built initially without shops, amenities or services, and second there was very little employment

directly to hand. . . . Various Residents Associations were set up to address these problems, and progress was very slow.[13]

The area has improved recently, as more and more residents bought and renovated their own homes, and then the city center was renovated from 1999 through 2002, which included the provision of shops and other amenities. The main streets are locked up at night in order to prevent vandalism, something that has plagued the area for years. There is now an ongoing plan in place for the further regeneration of the area over the next ten to fifteen years that will restore it to the original concept of a "garden city."

A group of elderly ladies who were concerned with the spiritual plight and social problems of young people and their families had been praying for the area for a number of years. Their prayers began to be answered when in 1992 a Christian music group that called itself the Worldwide Message Tribe began reaching out to the young people of the area on the streets and in the schools. The group, including Cameron Dante (a one-time disc jockey with BBC Radio One), frontman Andy Hawthorne (now CEO of The Message), and friend Mark Pennells, among others, had a passion to make the gospel relevant to young people. They found their beloved dance and hip-hop music was the best medium to communicate with kids in school. So they changed their name to the Message in 2000. The music group was formed to establish contact with the youth of Manchester through rap and popular dance, which in a short space of time became hugely popular.[14] The group later became known simply as the Tribe. For twelve years this group, under its various names, visited hundreds of Manchester high schools and performed concerts for well over one million people.

It was out of this music initiative that a family of youth ministries called the Message Trust emerged in 2000, giving rise to a number of events and initiatives, including Eden and Festival: Manchester. But in 2006, the Tribe, working under the umbrella of the Message Trust, decided to call it quits as a musical group and instead to invest their energies into the training of the next generation. They would do this through a program called Genetik,[15] "a state-of-the-art environment for creativity and inspiration to invest in a new generation of gifted artists and musicians. The Academy will offer the highest standard of facilities for a wide range of creative classes and courses through which young people can grow in life and faith."[16]

The challenge that the Message encountered was the difficulty of maintaining contact with the many young people who had responded to their message presentations in schools and concerts. They became convinced that they needed an ongoing presence within the community. The Eden Project was birthed in response to this need, working to develop "projects which help people to move from decision making to discipleship."[17]

They recognize that the challenge of reaching urban young people, focusing on those between the ages of eleven and eighteen who are marginalized in society and beyond the reach of many churches, requires extreme measures. Such is their passion that they declare, "We'll do anything to see young people reached for Jesus. Ideas which to others might seem outrageous, dangerous or just plain ridiculous make perfect sense when you're driven by a godly obsession."[18]

Since the inception of the Wythenshawe project, other partnerships have been launched in the Salford, Longsight, Openshaw, Swinton, Hattersley, and Failsworth districts of Greater Manchester. Currently there are ten Eden Partnerships in operation, each of which differs according to the needs of the community.

In 2000, Message 2000 oversaw the work of ten thousand "young Christian volunteers . . . in partnership with Greater Manchester churches on social, environmental, and crime reduction projects. This included a project on Swinton Valley estate formally known as 'the Bronx.' During ten days of work on the estate, according to police reports, there were no recorded incidents of crime, and since the summer of 2000, there has been a sustained 43 percent reduction in crime."[19]

In Salford, after consultations with parents and social workers, a LifeCentre was opened to offer facilities and activities for young people in the community. In a 2001 project called Urban Adventure, "eight hundred Christian young people cleared up six hundred tons of rubbish and refurbished two local youth centers, and as a result a sustained 14 percent reduction in crime was achieved." In 2005 the Big Deal was launched in Salford. "Pioneered by the Greater Manchester police and the Message, the Big Deal is a major community regeneration project, centered on transforming and regenerating communities. The Big Deal unites local communities, schools, churches, public service providers and private enterprise, making a coherent contribution to the long-term prosperity and security of the city and all those who live and work in it."[20]

In 2003, Festival: Manchester took place. "The Message was a key partner in this event, which drew over five thousand Christian young people who worked across the region." A community celebration at which evangelist Luis Palau spoke drew a large and enthusiastic crowd. Around two thousand of the young people worked on 130 police projects, "with a total of 317 projects completed." This gave rise to Festival: London two years later, including many cleanup projects around Greater London and climaxing in a gathering in Trafalgar Square in the heart of the city, with the enthusiastic support of political and civic leaders.[21]

The Eden Bus project was launched with the aid of the Greater Manchester police and local schools. They provide mobile youth centers and a safe, supervised environment, which together have had a considerable effect in reducing crime and anti-social behavior. The Message also partners with Youth for Christ in working with young offenders through the northwest's Young Offenders Institutes and has played a role in the creation and ongoing work of LifeCentre (a funky youth café environment, mentioned above), Genetik (a £1 million music, dance, and recording complex), and Reflex (which offers accredited programs delivered to young offenders in custody and operates across northwest England).

Our description so far has focused on the many activities of Eden Partnerships, but this need not overshadow the fact that their approach seeks to be holistic in terms of relating to the needs of young people, beyond simply providing activities for them to participate in. There is a vital spiritual basis to their ministry, which is expressed in the Breathe concept. In its work with young people who have had little or no exposure to the Christian message or involvement in church programs, Breathe provides a unique, "three-dimensional" approach to discipleship: breathe in your mind (through mentoring); breathe in your body (through volunteering); and breathe in your soul (through worship).[22]

Looking back over its twelve years of operation, the Message gives thanks to God that

> every day, we really are seeing young people transforming their lives and challenged communities turning around. We have helped to raise the self esteem of tens of thousands of local teenagers. We have helped to reduce crime in a number of difficult neighborhoods (including one estate in Salford where crime declined by over 40%). We have provided opportunities for thousands of young people to get involved in local volunteering. We also received a "Highly Commended" award at the prestigious national Charity Awards 2006.[23]

Their work has found favor with many local organizations that engage the problems of the inner city and have witnessed firsthand the lasting impact of the Eden Partnerships.

• Hope 2008 (United Kingdom) •

In the previous chapter we mentioned briefly the Hope 2008 initiative, in which local churches across the United Kingdom are invited to become involved in social action and service to their communities in the name of Christ. The Message in fact organized this national mission in partnership with many leading Christian charities and denominations. It was launched at the National Exhibition Center in Birmingham.

Hope 2008 is an initiative of the churches of Britain and Ireland that is working to demonstrate Christian faith in action and to explain the meaning of that faith wherever the opportunity arises. This multifaceted initiative has the support of both national and local political leaders, the police, as well as church leaders from the principal religious communities.

On June 11, 2008, a select group of Hope 2008 volunteers were invited to meet Prince Charles to tell him about acts of kindness they had been involved in. Addressing the group, Prince Charles said, "I have been fascinated going around talking to all of you today, and I hope I have met everybody, to hear about how 'Hope08' started and how it has spread, and what a marvelous response it has received all over this country."[24] In addressing the group, he expressed admiration for the initiative and acknowledged both the need for a cooperative service venture among young people and the value of reconnecting with the "sense of the sacred" in nature.

Hope 2008 did not consist of events that were centrally planned, but instead was made up of hundreds of local initiatives that were registered online so that anyone could see at a glance what activities were taking place in their particular location. The Christian Enquiry Agency and Church Army set up a Web site (www.HopeInfo.co.uk) in support of this initiative, offering a wide range of ideas to help stimulate creative initiatives, such as setting up winter shelters for the homeless; lobbying for the retention of postal and other services threatened with closure in villages; worship and teaching events; and many others. A number of locations have generated their own blogs in order to exchange news of what is happening in their area.

I was especially fascinated to see that racing driver Hector Lester, who is a member of Christians in Motorsport, has included the Hope 2008 logo on his Ferrari 430, which he races as part of the GT3 league. His performance in each race is recorded online for fans, who are encouraged to check out the latest race results and turn out to support him as he races on circuits around the country. Hector and his team welcome the involvement of local churches at each of his racing events and can be contacted through the Hope 2008 office.[25]

Looking back at 2008, it has been encouraging to see how churches of many denominations and many independent congregations have worked together in such a wide variety of projects in towns and villages across the land.

A Decentralized "Cluster" Approach

A growing number of churches are moving from a centralized approach to a more network-oriented approach involving clusters or mid-sized communities, in order to develop an ever-increasing number of neighborhood-based faith communities. These groups should not be thought of as fellowship-based home groups, nor are they independent house churches; each cluster is a full-fledged church, while at the same time relating to other clusters as part of a larger identity with shared vision and values.

Bob Hopkins describes the cluster philosophy in *Clusters*, a book co-authored with Mike Breen. The cluster model is designed to structure the church around the core belief that God intends people to live out their faith in communities of fellow believers within their own cultural context. Hopkins and Breen believe that the cluster concept can help unlock the clericalism, consumerism, and come-to-us mentality that have crippled the ongoing mission of the church.

> To understand clusters we shall need to recognize that one of the principal weaknesses of the western church is that we have lost Biblical and sociological "congregation." What we now call congregation, we believe is something different. This is particularly serious because we define church as congregation and it's the word congregation that carries all our assumptions about church.[26]

Churches in urban contexts can best engage the wider community by providing multiple entry points through a decentralized structure comprised of clusters. Each cluster is defined and shaped by its missional calling, which provides its distinctive ethos. The cluster concept is not simply a restructuring of a large church, which in many instances has become an alternative method of control to keep pace with numerical growth. To the contrary, clusters represent low hierarchical control with high peer accountability. The cluster is defined not by so much by its ecclesial identity as by the missional vocation that defines each one, setting them apart while also holding them together and giving them motivation.

The cluster is a mid-sized group that may or may not consist of a number of cell groups. Its size ideally is between thirty and fifty, which is small enough to provide intimacy and accountability, yet large enough to allow for a range of gifts and experience to help implement its missional vision. In other words, clusters are "small enough to share a common vision and large enough to do something about it."[27] The cluster is not just a gathering of neighbors, but is a grouping with a specific sociological, ecclesiological, and missional identity. Clusters also provide contexts in which new social groups can be identified and from which tailor-made clusters can emerge and grow.

Hopkins and Breen are at pains to emphasize that clusters are fully church, expressing their corporate life in three dimensions: "upward" in worship, which may embrace the liturgical or be entirely spontaneous; "inward" in discipleship, expressing hospitality, care, prayer, and financial help; and "outward" in mission, listening to their chosen context to identify the needs, aspirations, and social patterns.[28] They summarize the role of clusters as a place of identity, belonging, and ownership; a point of gathering; a context for training; and to generate embryos for further church plants.[29]

The authors recognize that decentralization is prone to lead to fragmentation unless the clusters are linked together by strong bonds. The following components are identified as providing the "glue" that holds the clusters together around a common purpose:

- P = Purpose—mission focus
- V = Values—community qualities
- A = Agreed Language—name and story

In describing this glue as the shared mission purpose, community values, and associated language, we were not only recognizing common characteristics developing in most clusters. The increasingly strong evidence was that the clearer these were and the better they were communicated and owned (helped by the agreed language), the more vigorous and healthy was the cluster.[30]

The development of healthy cluster life can also be greatly aided by the use of "LifeShapes" as an operating system, where each of eight different shapes represents an aspect of discipleship to be incorporated as a life skill: the learning *circle* enables individuals to identify God's interventions in their daily life; the *semi-circle* describes the ark of a pendulum swing, representing the essential rhythm of rest and work; the *triangle*, with its three points, identifies the essential "upward," "inward," and "outward" dimensions of a balanced life; the four sides of the *square* represent the stages in leadership development; the *pentagon* translates the language of the fivefold ministry, identified in Ephesians, of apostle, prophet, evangelist, pastor, and teacher and helps the cluster to develop ministry in each of these callings; the *hexagon* encourages the development of a life of prayer based on the structure of the Lord's Prayer; the *heptagon* applies the seven signposts of biological life (movement, respiration, sensitivity, growth, reproduction, excretion, and nutrition) to the spiritual realm; and finally, the *octagon* describes the elements of mission.[31] The LifeShapes strategy may be regarded as a reinterpretation and elaboration of the classic spiritual disciplines within contemporary settings, but it should not be regarded as a program or course to be completed. Rather, it serves as an operating system that provides the DNA for the church and needs to be constantly revisited.

At the time of writing, a network of fifteen churches is at work developing the cluster model, sharing insights and monitoring progress regularly through chat rooms and an annual conference. These churches are for the most part within, but are not strictly confined to, mainstream denominations. Early results show that with the development of clusters, or mid-sized communities, comes greater evangelistic effectiveness. Through 3 Dimension Ministries, the model is also being field tested in six churches across the United States and in nine additional churches in England, Norway, Denmark, Finland, and Switzerland.[32]

One incarnation of the cluster approach is the simple church movement, which has its roots in the older house church movement but is distinctive not in terms of *where* individual churches meet but rather in terms of its attempts at redefining *what* church is: namely, a Christ-centered community that is based on mutual relationships and expressed in worship, fellowship, and service. It is "church" stripped of the nonessentials, meeting without specially trained clergy, buildings, regalia, formal liturgy, and programs. And it is "simple" in that it is deliberately kept small in order to ensure maximum participation and flexibility. Worship and mission are inseparably linked, an emphasis that we will explore in the final chapter. Sometimes other terms are used to describe the movement, including "organic church," "essential church," and "primitive church."[33]

While the simple church concept provides the opportunity for exponential growth, its lack of connectivity, both historically with the Christian tradition and outwardly with other networks of churches, has the potential to lead to isolationism and judgmental attitudes. In order to counteract such consequences, an alternative approach would be to express the simple church concept within a historic Christian tradition and as part of a linked network, thus ensuring accountability beyond the individual small group.

• St. Thomas' Crookes and the Philadelphia Center • (Sheffield, England)

In the United Kingdom, St. Thomas' Crookes, together with its citywide Philadelphia Center ministries, is a parish church that has taken a more decentralized approach in recent years, utilizing the cluster model of mid-sized communities. St. Thomas' testifies that the shortage of leaders is the most common and critical limitation in churches. They "release a leadership explosion" for effective outreach by which new churches can be seeded.[34] The Sheffield-based clusters of the St. Thomas campuses are serving students, young adults, creators, vulnerable people, business communities, families, the elderly, local communities, and more. Their model is being examined and replicated as each year churches from throughout the United Kingdom and across Europe, Australia, New Zealand, and North America visit to learn from their experience.

• St. Andrew's Chorleywood (Hertfordshire, England) •

St. Andrew's Chorleywood provides another example of a church that currently has twenty-six clusters, which they call "mid-sized groups."[35] The church decentralized during a nine-month period when the church building was being remodeled and it was not possible to worship there. At that time, the church scattered into nineteen clusters, and when the remodeling was complete it was no longer large enough to accommodate the numbers. They now have twenty-six clusters and three church plants, two within the community of Chorleywood and one in Watford. The Watford church is called Soul

Survivor, which also became the springboard for an international youth network of the same name.[36]

• Trinity Cheltenham (Cheltenham, England) •

Trinity Cheltenham is another church that has embraced the cluster concept. Under the leadership of Mark Bailey, the church decentralized in 2004 into seventy-six small church groups, with nineteen clusters, each looked after by "cluster parents."[37] Trinity is a vibrant town-center Anglican church that has broken free from a traditional parochial mindset. It combines weekly celebrative worship with an ongoing commitment to manifold expressions of service and witness through its cluster network. Trinity's introductory course on the Christian faith is based on the Alpha program and introduces inquirers to a small group format at the outset. Upon completion of the course they move on to the clusters for further spiritual growth and ministry involvement.

• Pantego Bible Church (Arlington, Texas) •

In the North American context, Pantego Bible Church in Arlington, Texas, followed the lead of pastor Randy Frazee in implementing a grand vision of establishing the presence of Jesus in every neighborhood where members of the church were located. During a ten-year period starting in 1990, the church turned from being in decline to experiencing fivefold growth. A decentralized approach to ministry and mission was at the heart of this congregational revitalization, as they came to the realization that their small group strategy was not working and that they had to explore "the characteristics that drive successful experience of community." The radical conclusion they eventually came to was that *"biblical community is the life of Christ on earth today."*[38]

• Trinity Grace Church (New York, New York) •

Although unrelated to 3 Dimension Ministries, Trinity Grace Church is following a similar strategy. It has launched a number of neighborhood churches as a decentralized outreach around the city. These churches, like the Sheffield model, are made up of mid-sized missional communities of between thirty and fifty people, each centered on a shared mission to a neighborhood or industry. Every community has an outreach component that involves them in serving, praying, and working alongside other people, seeking to build solid, lasting relationships fostered by common interests. Such communities, along with the "lifegroups" of five to twelve individuals that are the even smaller building blocks of the missional communities, make the church readily accessible by offering multiple points of entry into Trinity Grace Church.[39]

The Multicultural Dimension

To the extent that urban emerging churches are genuinely missional, they will become multicultural both in membership and leadership. Urban churches become elitist "bubbles" or alien enclaves when they consist primarily either of whites who have fled the city, only to return to support the church in the localities in which they were raised, or of a culturally homogeneous group of people who have moved into the city. Within tight-knit urban neighborhoods, the local people distinguish between those they know in their homegrown community groups and those outsiders who do not really belong.

The under-35s who have grown up in multicultural, urban environments have attended school and college where Caucasians are increasingly in the minority. They socialize, date, and marry cross-culturally. This mix will eventually be reflected in the urban church community, unless the church has a segregationist mentality. However, racial and ethnic lines continue to divide many urban communities, creating invisible barriers behind which gangs defend their respective territories.

Some communities assimilate, while others colonize, banding together in order to preserve their language, culture, and religion. Orthodox Jews populate areas that are in close proximity to their synagogue and the shops that provide kosher food, and conservative Muslims colonize areas that are near their shops, coffee houses, and mosque. Some racial groups assimilate more rapidly than others.

Cities that have attracted waves of immigrants from different parts of the world now boast their own Chinatowns, Koreatowns, Little Tokyos, Little Saigons, and Hispanic Barrios, among others.

As Christians embrace the comprehensive message of the gospel of the reign of Christ, so they learn to celebrate the contributions made by different ethnic groups, instead of seeing differences as a threat. Latinos, East Africans, and Pacific Islanders demonstrate the warmth of relationships. African-Americans and Africans release joyful celebration and freedom of movement in worship. The Korean community demonstrates its commitment to corporate intercessory prayer and its musical genius. Christians who come as refugees to the West from other areas of the world teach us grace and fortitude in the face of persecution. And this list could go on—but it is illustrative of the rich tapestry of cultural diversity and Christian experience that can enrich the church and save us from monocultural monotony.

In response to this complex scenario, we would expect to see Christian faith communities birthed within each group, while at the same time expressing the reconciling power of the gospel in reaching across ethnic and cultural divides. Freedom in the gospel enables us to celebrate diversity, overcoming prejudice and fear of those who are different from ourselves. In regard to the North American context, Tom Sine challenges the churches in the United States to wake up to the fact that "by 2060 the United States will become the first non-European western nation—a nation of Latinos, African-Americans and Asians."[40] Tommy Kyllonen reminds us that "the emerging church is also the young black male in the hood. It is the second generation Mexican in Los Angeles and the child of the Chinese immigrant in Houston. The emerging church is the Puerto Rican female in Wall Street."[41] With such a kaleidoscope of cultures, we should expect to see a rich diversity of church life expressed.

Principally serving urban blacks, hip-hop churches are emerging to engage young people who are not attracted to the traditional form of service. They seek to reconnect to black young people who have been enticed away by popular culture and gang allegiance. According to a *Religion & Ethics* cover story in 2005, there were at that time about 150 churches relating to the hip-hop culture.[42]

• Greater Hood Memorial AME Zion Church •
(New York, New York)

One example is the Hip Hop Church, located at Greater Hood Memorial AME Zion Church. Their hip-hop church choir and several of the rappers also minister at Friday night FLAYVA (Freedom, Love and Abundant Youth Victory Alliance) worship services in the Greater New York area. Their mission, as described for visitors to their Web site, is

> to present the Christian gospel in a setting that appeals to both those individuals who are confessed Christians as well as those who are considered unchurched. The Hip Hop Church is worship and scriptural study. The Hip Hop Church is outreach out to the disenfranchised, the brokenhearted, the oppressed and those considered "disposable" by the larger society. Our worship services follow an order of service consistent with many African-American churches, while always allowing the Holy Spirit to have full reign. "Hip Hop is the culture, while Jesus is the Center." . . .
>
> The Hip Hop Church is Here!!! In the spirit of the announced ministry of Jesus Christ (Luke 4:18) and in the Spirit of Paul's calling to minister to all men, women, boys and girls (1 Cor. 9:19–22), we are presenting the Gospel of Jesus Christ through the contemporary culture of the Hip Hop Generation. Our goal is to bring young men and women to Christ, no matter how they may seem to the outside world. Rev. Stephen Pogue, Pastor of Greater Hood Memorial AME Zion, says "Just because (young people) wear clothes a certain way doesn't mean they are the way they look. They can still follow a lifestyle of holiness, of trying to be right and righteous. They want to be able to listen to the music they want to listen to and still say 'There's nothing wrong with me.'"
>
> We minister to God's People presenting a viable option to the profanity, misogyny, violence and foolishness that most of us are force-fed daily. We encourage the members of the Hip Hop Church to sing, dance and express themselves in any way that the Spirit of God moves them. We honor straight A students, students who have overcome adversity, community leaders, church leaders and some of the unsung pioneers of Hip Hop each week, in line with the biblical admonishment to "Love one another with mutual affection; outdo one another in showing honor" (Romans 12:10).[43]

• Lawndale Community Church (Chicago, Illinois) •

Chicago's Lawndale district, an economically impoverished area that is predominantly African American, is the home of Lawndale Community Church. Wayne Gordon, an Anglo graduate of Wheaton College and Northern Baptist Theological Seminary, moved to North Lawndale in 1975 to work as a teacher and coach at Farragut High School, also located in North Lawndale, and founded the church in 1978. Today Lawndale Community Church has over one thousand worshiping families, and Wayne continues as pastor. As a church, their commitment is to both the Great Commandment—"to love the Lord with all our heart, soul, mind, and strength and to love our neighbors as ourselves (Matt. 22:37–39)"—and the Great Commission, to make disciples of all nations (Matt. 28:19–20). Their commitment is both personal and communal. "At the heart of our ministry is our commitment to compassionately renew lives and revitalize our community."[44]

In the church's early years, 45 percent of the local population lived below the poverty line and 26 percent were unemployed. So in 1984 the church founded the Lawndale Christian Health Center, which now sees over 120,000 patients a year. It also launched the Lawndale Christian Development Corporation in 1987 to bring holistic revitalization to the lives and environments of Lawndale residents through housing improvements, educational enrichment, and community advocacy. Lawndale Community Church also hosts a hip-hop church that reaches out to the youth of the community.

Pastor Wayne Gordon is affectionately known as "Coach." As lead pastor he has surrounded himself with a leadership team that is predominantly African American. One of his major goals has been to develop a new generation of leaders for North Lawndale, a goal that has started to be realized as many young people have graduated from college and are returning to live and work in North Lawndale. President George Bush gave Lawndale Community Church a "Point of Light" award in 1989, and Chicago Magazine named Wayne one of the Chicagoans of the year in 1995 for his commitment and creativity.[45]

Lawndale Community Church can testify to the exciting and even remarkable ways that God is at work in their community: "There are many things happening in North Lawndale that we have never seen before. Hundreds of new homes are being built, development is everywhere, [and] there is even a Starbucks in our community! We at Lawndale Community Church are excited to be here 'For Such A Time As This.' "[46]

Lawndale Community Church's example demonstrates clearly that urban engagement entails a multipronged approach, meeting people on their "turf" in situations in which they feel relaxed. Such a strategy requires the use of different kinds of venues, such as cafés, coffee bars, pubs, schools, community centers, business premises, and fitness centers. Sometimes these locations represent simply a place for conversation; at other times they are the home base of a faith community. They may even represent businesses that are operated by Christians who have a desire to demonstrate the application of kingdom values in the marketplace.

• Glorious Undead (London, England) •

Glorious Undead is associated with the Elim Network in the United Kingdom, a Pentecostal denomination that grew out of the Welsh Revival of 1904. Glorious Undead describes itself as

> a Christian church based in London UK doing our best to live in a Christ like way (see Mark 12:30–31). A lot of us are involved in our local alternative music scenes (rock, industrial, punk, hardcore, metal, goth, rockabilly, acoustic etc.) but there are no prerequisites! Everyone is welcome at GU. We do not follow religion but follow Jesus and his example with a true faith and bible based theology, [and] we are overseen by the Elim network and run by volunteers.[47]

Glorious Undead relates particularly well to the people of Kentish Town, an inner London location where significant numbers of Goths gather. At the time of publication, their Web site provides photos of some three hundred registered friends, a testament to the extent of their appeal to the youth counterculture.

• Quest Church (Seattle, Washington) •

Quest Church is "an urban, multigenerational, and multiethnic church in Seattle, striving to be an incarnational presence in a post-modern and postchurch culture."[48] They are committed to being a seven-day-a-week church, ministering to the whole person and reaching out to the community by demonstrating compassion and a commitment to social justice. In keeping with the culture of the area they have created Q Café as a gathering place. Through this non-profit, non-religious café, they endeavor to put their theology into daily incarnation. They wanted to explore the viability of operating successfully by applying kingdom values in the marketplace. They raise the following pertinent questions:

> Is it possible to serve direct trade [fair trade] coffee and tea and dem-onstrate care for our environment and coffee farmers? Is it possible to create a unique venue where not only would people enjoy incredible coffee but be connected to the larger community? Is it possible to create a space where local artists and musicians would have a platform to share their unique talents? Is it possible to create a venue where children, parents, college students, local businesspeople, the homeless, and senior citizens can all come to enjoy a neighborhood cafe?[49]

Q Café endeavors to develop a replicating model where profits would go towards supporting classes, providing resources for the home-less, programs for children, and rental space for neighbors and local non-profits. This is what they have achieved to date:

> Since its inception from 2002, Q Cafe is making its mark. In ad-dition to write-ups in the Seattle Weekly and the Seattle Times, it was also named one of the best independent cafes in the country by Worthwhile Magazine. It has hosted countless local musicians through shows and open mic in addition to national musicians such as Tyrone Wells, Smoosh and Nickelcreek. Every 4–6 weeks, local artists adorn the walls with their expressions. Hundreds of homeless men and women have been helped through the resources we collect in partnership with Quest Church's "To the Streets" program. Two families were given an opportunity to be placed into permanent hous-ing. Over $10,000 has been raised thus far for benevolent and justice

causes like the Tsunami Fund, AIDS, etc. Q Café is also committed to giving 10% of all café sales to local and global non-profit causes. The space is used by local businesses, neighborhood groups, AA meetings, churches, other non-profits, moms' group, and rented for all purposes—even weddings. Q Cafe is growing into a community presence . . .[50]

Resources for Local Churches

As Western churches increasingly engage in cross-cultural mission in response to the pluralistic makeup of their societies, they are recognizing the need to gain fresh insights and learn new skills. They are turning to those mission agencies that have many years of experience in evangelization, community service, and church planting in areas of the world in which the church has learned to witness from the margins of society. They are also enlisting the support of agencies that have focused on various aspects of mission in the West. There was a time when church and so-called parachurch existed in a competitive relationship; thankfully, their somewhat antagonistic attitude toward one another is giving way to one of mutual affirmation and collaboration.

• Mosaic (Los Angeles, California) •

Mosaic now meets in five locations in Greater Los Angeles; with each relating to a contrasting social context, their very name describes their diversity. Yet each of the congregations shares a common vision to be "a community of followers of Jesus Christ, committed to live by faith, to be known by love, and to be a voice of hope." The name Mosaic also symbolizes "a broken and fragmented humanity which can become a work of beauty under the artful hands of God." They welcome people "from all walks of life, regardless of where they are in their spiritual journey," to come together and discover how their lives can fit together. Like a jigsaw puzzle, the pieces only make sense when they are in right relationship with other pieces.[51]

The influence of Mosaic is spread widely both through the vision of Erwin McManus, a gifted speaker and author, and through the

Mosaic Alliance, "a global network committed to create the future by unleashing a culture of entrepreneurship, activism, innovation, authenticity, and creativity within the local church." The Alliance seeks "to empower and equip churches and leaders to maximize the creative potential in the communities in which they serve," with a particular emphasis on serving church planters.[52]

Growing churches in urban contexts are increasingly multiracial, challenging the long-held assumption that homogeneous churches are the most numerically strong. This transition may reflect a shift from predominantly first to now second and subsequent generations that have become progressively integrated. This does not mean that they have blended into a host culture, but rather that they have created their own multicultural identity. Within the Evangelical Covenant Church, for example, 50 percent of their new missional church plants are ethnic or multicultural.[53]

Especially among urban young people, there is a strong reaction against churches that have bought into the so-called health and wealth gospel, with its emphasis on God's provision of material prosperity and physical well-being for his followers. They also tend to walk away from authoritarian and celebrity-focused churches, and they want to see church leaders living out the servant leadership model that was best exemplified by Jesus. This trend is evident not just among young whites but also among blacks and Asians.

• Church Resource Ministries •

Church Resource Ministries (CRM) has gained high regard for its assistance to churches by coming alongside to listen to issues raised by churches as experienced in their ministry contexts and to work collaboratively to find ways to address these issues. Their approaches are as varied as the situations they encounter in more than twenty countries in a wide variety of contexts. Across North America it serves leaders, churches and denominations to equip the American church to engage its increasingly secular society. "No fluff, no hype, no gimmicks. Just seasoned leaders who walk with God and with leaders like you, helping them engage a complex world."[54] They recognize the missional challenges presented by a North America that is an increasingly postmodern society. The urban environment is becoming increasingly diverse and complex so that churches cannot simply use imported church models and prepackaged strategies. With urban contexts they are committed to supporting and developing multicultural churches in order to reflect the cultural diversity of the communities in which they are located and model the reconciling power of the gospel. Urban churches that demonstrate their ability to develop cross-cultural respect and understanding to the point of celebrating diversity have a huge potential for growth.

In order to address these concerns CRM has developed a ministry called Urban Mosaic, which is designed to help strengthen and develop multicultural churches through the coaching of pastors, leaders, and church planters who are trying to develop churches that reach and reflect the diverse communities in which they find themselves. Their strategy is to support those who are intentionally beginning multicultural church plants, as well as churches that are presently monocultural but that are seeking to transition into multiethnic ministry. To this end, they help multicultural teams learn to work together, celebrating their diversity and developing mutual understanding, while ultimately demonstrating the reconciling and transforming power of the gospel.

Urban Mosaic is inspired by a vision "to catalyze a movement of multicultural churches in every major urban area in North America."[55] They believe that as this happens, the North American church will begin to truly model what Martin Luther King Jr. referred to as the "Beloved Community," and in so doing it will move to its God-mandated place at the forefront of the fight for racial reconciliation and social and economic justice in our broken and fractured society. They believe that every local church is called to the ministry of reconciliation (2 Cor. 5:18–19) and to remove barriers that separate people, rather than erect them (Eph. 2:11–22).

Many other ministries with an emphasis on urban areas could be cited in this discussion, including the urban projects that are run by InterVarsity Christian Fellowship and serve in nearly thirty cities around the United States,[56] as well as World Impact, which describes itself as "a Christian missions organization dedicated to ministering God's love in the inner cities of America . . . through evangelism, follow-up, discipleship and church planting."[57] The list could go on at great length.[58]

Summary

In this chapter we have only been able to skim the surface to indicate the range of urban engagement that is currently taking place. The examples are impressive in their diversity, in terms of the churches and organizations responding to the cry of the city, as well as the different approaches and the social and ethnic groups that are being embraced in these endeavors.

The extent of their commitment—that so many are there for the long haul—is impressive. This is no hit-and-run approach, but a deep-level identification with the cultural context, often at great personal cost. And yet there is a total absence of martyr complex. Their sense of the call of God is so strong and clear that the individuals and groups involved would choose to be no place else. They regard the neighborhoods where they live as home and the people they serve as more than friends; they are their brothers and sisters in whom they discover the presence of Christ.

It is worth noting that many of the urban churches included in our survey represent indigenous expressions of church. They are faith communities that have been *birthed* within their neighborhoods and are therefore culturally appropriate to their contexts; they do not represent preconceived church models that are *planted* by outside agencies and groups. Urban contexts are so diverse that faith communities will have to discover what "church" will look like for them, enabling them to express worship, embody fellowship, and engage in ongoing mission to their wider community. In the following chapter, we will continue the urban theme when we consider the contribution of the new resurgent monasticism.

6

resurgent monasticism

Throughout the long history of the church, the monastic orders have performed a strategic role in establishing new faith, especially on the frontiers of Christendom. Those same communities have also contributed significantly to the renewal of the spiritual lives of many Christians and congregations within Christendom contexts. Northern Europe was evangelized through the Celtic monastic communities, which were established in Ireland by the sixth century. The monastic tradition has continued mainly among Roman Catholics and the Orthodox, but Anglican and Lutheran orders were later established, as these Reformation churches came to recognize that they had become somewhat spiritually impoverished, and seriously missionally hampered, by the dissolution of the monasteries.

In recent decades the monastic tradition has garnered wider appeal, especially among the increasing numbers of evangelicals reacting against the activism and spiritual shallowness of many of their churches. Their hunger for a deeper spirituality and authentic relationships, and their desire to reconnect with the ancient forms of worship, has drawn them to the monastic tradition. They began their engagement with monasticism by making retreats in existing communities in increasing numbers. More recently they have begun to form their own monastic and missional orders. Tom Sine provides a concise description of the New Monasticism.

> Most of the groups in the monastic stream have no interest in church planting. While large numbers of twenty- and thirty-year-olds are involved, it is comprised of a larger number of the over-forty crowd than the other three streams [emerging, missional, and mosaic]. It is also significantly more multicultural and multinational than the emerging and missional streams.[1]

Although still numerically small, involving an estimated two thousand people in community living, the New Monasticism is attracting increasing attention among evangelicals of all ages. It is a movement that, according to Jonathan Wilson-Hartgrove, seeks to awaken the churches of North America to the question of "what it means to be Christians as citizens of the world's last remaining superpower at the beginning of the third millennium."[2]

Wilson-Hartgrove believes, as does the movement he represents, that the church in the West has lost its way, having succumbed to the economic and cultural pressures of consumerism and become debilitated by the fragmentation caused by the undermining of community and loss of social roots. He states, "So many Christians in America today feel paralyzed by the paradox of a church that promises so much yet seems so hard to find in reality."[3]

In response to the increasingly dysfunctional nature of modern society, the church must become not only a countercultural movement, but also an incarnational presence, in its endeavor to re-establish authentic community. "How can the church live faithfully in a fragmented world as a minority culture?" is a question that needs to be addressed as a matter of urgency.[4] Western Christians will have to face, as they seldom have before, the reality of costly discipleship as they challenge the presuppositions of a society whose values are at variance with those of the reign of God.

New Monasticism is described as "a grassroots ecumenism and prophetic witness" that represents a number of concerns and commitments. An assembly of leaders meeting at Rutba House, in association with St. John's Baptist Church in Durham, North Carolina, identifies the following characteristics:

- Relocation to the abandoned places of Empire
- Sharing economic resources with fellow community members and the needy among us
- Hospitality to the stranger
- Lament for racial divisions within the church and our communities combined with the active pursuit of a just reconciliation
- Humble submission to Christ's body, the church
- Intentional formation in the way of Christ and the rule of the community along the lines of the old novitiate
- Nurturing common life among members of intentional community
- Support for celibate singles alongside monogamous married couples and their children
- Geographical proximity to community members who share a common rule of life
- Care for the plot of God's earth given to us along with support of our local economies
- Peacemaking in the midst of violence and conflict resolution within communities along the lines of Matthew 18
- Commitment to a disciplined contemplative life[5]

Contemporary monasticism has three expressions: renewal and reconciliation, incarnational ministries among the poor, and those engaged in birthing new faith communities. Many communities embody more than one of these expressions.

Renewal and Reconciliation

The first expression of the Resurgent Monasticism consists of communities committed to a ministry of renewal through meditation and the practice of spiritual disciplines. This tradition goes back to the Egyptian desert fathers of the third century; these individuals sought to deepen their awareness of God through extended periods of solitude in the desert. Early in the fourth century, some of the solitary monks began to organize themselves into communities. During the Middle Ages, the monastic communities began to establish houses where they could live out their calling in urban contexts. They endeavored to meet the pressing spiritual and social needs of the people who looked to them for guidance and support.

Today, contemplative orders provide a corrective to the hyperactivism and materialism of contemporary Western societies. They are oases of calm and repose that are proving immensely popular with people seeking to wind down and refocus, as they make time to recover from their adrenaline addiction. Christian people, drawn from a surprising variety of traditions, attend retreats within monastic communities, often in pursuit of this sort of renewal.

Jonathan Wilson-Hartgrove, a founding member of Rutba House and leading spokesperson for the New Monasticism, links renewal and relocation, arguing that we often need a new setting in order to gain a fresh perspective. For some, this has entailed a costly uprooting and establishment of a new permanent home in community with other Christians who share the same vision. For many, this will not mean living communally, but rather as near neighbors. He also suggests that members of traditional churches might relocate some of their activities from church premises or their own homes in order to share with troubled inner-city teens, for example, or to be with men in a local prison.[6] He observes that when we open the Scripture in company with people in unfamiliar settings and with different experiences of life from our own, they raise questions that we may not have addressed before and bring a fresh perspective on familiar biblical texts.

• Evangelical Sisterhood of Mary (Darmstadt, Germany) •

Some communities were birthed to pray for and demonstrate reconciliation in situations of ethnic conflict and racial tensions. During and after the Second World War, a number of such communities came into existence. Among them was the Evangelical

Sisterhood of Mary in Darmstadt, Germany, which was founded in 1947 within the German Evangelical Church but now has branches in many parts of the world.[7] The Sisterhood has houses in the United States, Canada, Brazil, Australia, Paraguay, the United Kingdom, Finland, Holland, Japan, Norway, and South Africa.

Even before the outbreak of World War II, Mother Basilea (Dr. Klara Schlink) defied the Hitler regime by refusing to bow to the Nazi party's demands that Jewish Christians should be barred from meetings. "During World War II she risked her life and career by speaking publicly on the unique destiny of God's people, Israel. Summoned twice before the Gestapo for proclaiming the lordship of Jesus Christ, she was allowed to go free in spite of her uncompromising stand." In like manner, Mother Martyria (Erika Madauss), the other founding mother of the order, "held Bible studies [during the war] for young people, even teaching them the Old Testament, which was forbidden under Hitler."[8]

The origins of the order go back to September 11, 1944, when Darmstadt was destroyed in an air raid in which over twelve thousand people were killed. That dreadful night was a time when the girls in a bible study led by Klara Schlink and Erika Madauss experienced the presence of God, leading them to repentance and the realization that lukewarm Christianity had to be replaced by genuine repentance and a passion for God. The order was inaugurated in 1947 with a special concern for the Jewish people and the survivors of the Holocaust, and an ongoing witness against every manifestation of anti-Semitism. Their communities are, to this day, places of prayer and of trust in God to supply all that is needed in daily life and in the realization of the vision of the order.

• The Ecumenical Monastic Community of Bose •
(Bose, Italy)

There are a numbers of orders that combine ecumenical concerns with spiritual renewal. A Catholic layman by the name of Enzo Bianchi established The Ecumenical Monastic Community of Bose, located between Milan and Turin, in 1965. It has become one of the most important religious foundations since Vatican II that is both ecumenical in membership and includes men and women.

• The Taizé Community (Normandy, France) •

The Taizé Community, named after the Normandy village where it is located, was founded by Brother Roger in 1940 and led by him until his sudden death under tragic circumstances in 2005.[9] The community attracts thousands of young people from around the world each year to weeklong retreats dedicated to worship, prayer, and meditation, designed to help the individual in his or her spiritual journey. Its contemplative songs with repetitive lyrics have proved popular in churches around the world, leading to the adoption of Taizé style worship, including chants, candles, and icons in many Protestant congregations, regardless of whether they have a tradition of liturgical worship. The Taizé Community seeks to be a catalyst for the renewal of individual Christians and local churches.

• The Iona Community (Scotland) •

"The Iona Community is a dispersed Christian ecumenical community working for peace and social justice, the rebuilding of community and the renewal of worship."[10] It has its main island centers on Iona and Mull off the west coast of Scotland, and its mainland home and administrative headquarters is located in Glasgow, where it works among youth and provides resources to revitalize the worship of local churches through Wild Goose Publications, representing a contemporary revival of Celtic spirituality. The movement was founded in 1938 by a Church of Scotland minister, the Reverend George MacLeod, working in the midst of economic depression in his dockland parish in Govan.

The Iona Abbey is a restored Benedictine house with accommodation for about fifty residents, but it also serves as a center for pilgrims and tourists.[11] The members of the Iona Community, though spread throughout the world, "share a common Rule which includes: daily prayer and reading the Bible; mutual sharing and accountability for our use of time and money; regular meeting together; and action and reflection for justice, peace and the integrity of creation." Members meet regularly throughout the year in local groups and in four plenary gatherings, including a week on Iona. They organize themselves into groups that share a variety of concerns relating to, among other things, "justice, peace and the integrity of creation (opposing nuclear weapons, campaigning against the arms trade and for ecological justice); political and cultural action to combat racism; action on local and global poverty and justice; issues in human sexuality; |and| the deepening of ecumenical dialogue and communion."[12]

• Lindisfarne Community (Ithaca, New York) •

The Lindisfarne Community identifies with the emerging church while also representing New Monasticism. They stress the fact that they are deeply rooted in historical Christianity and draw their inspiration from the Celtic tradition, while remaining open to input from other traditions. They seek to live a balanced life of prayer, study, service, and rest, as they explore new ways of being church appropriate for the twenty-first century. In their own words, they have "embraced emphases from, among others, the Celtic Christian communities of the fourth to ninth centuries in Northern Britain and Ireland; the desert fathers and mothers and the early monastic movement; the Christian mystics; the radicals of the sixteenth century; the charismatic, Christian feminist and home church movements of the twentieth."[13]

• Missio Dei (Minneapolis, Minnesota) •

Missio Dei is a small community that is rooted in the West Bank neighborhood of Minneapolis. It is a neo-monastic house made up of individuals who are seeking to follow the way of Jesus in a deeper way as they live out the gospel, which they describe as "the Jesus manifesto." They practice prayer, based on their own Missio Dei Breviary, with a message of God's peace, simplicity, and hospitality that they extend to the diverse neighborhood in which they live.

Unlike many other neo-monastic communities, they have a strong missional commitment to their local context and see themselves as being a part of God's mission on the West Bank. Rather than waiting for people to come to them, they are committed to going to the people wherever they are. Their faith is rooted in the ancient affirmations of the Nicene and Apostles' Creeds and is further summarized in their rule of life.

"We will center our lives on Jesus Christ.

- We will devote ourselves to a careful reading of the Gospel, going from Gospel to life and life to Gospel.
- We will actively seek to encounter the living and active person of Jesus Christ through the reading of Scripture and through prayer, trusting in the power of the Holy Spirit to shape us into the likeness of Jesus Christ.
- We will pursue a rhythm of morning and evening prayers.
- We will strive to live life with the people on the edges of society—the poor, the forsaken, the oppressed, and the disgraced.
- As Christ chose for himself a humble life, we will seek to live simply in our affluent culture of over-consumption.
- We will strive to purify our hearts from the desire for possession and power.
- Forsaking violence in all of its forms, we will seek and promote peaceful ways of resolving conflict.

"We will be present to the West Bank.

- We will spend time understanding the cultures of the West Bank.
- We will try to get in the way of injustice—particularly on the West Bank.
- We will intentionally build friendships with people on the West Bank.
- We will remember the people of the West Bank in our daily prayers.
- We will extend hospitality to our neighbors, sharing what we have with those in need—whether it is a simple meal, clothing, a place to sleep for the night, or our friendship.

"We share our lives with one another.

- We will seek to encounter the living and active person of Jesus Christ in our brothers and sisters.
- We will regularly attend Missio Dei's gatherings.

- We will regularly fellowship and pray with members of Missio Dei outside of formal gatherings.
- We will share resources with those within Missio Dei who demonstrate greater need.
- We will seek to intercede daily for the other members of Missio Dei.
- We will pursue reconciliation in our relationships with one another, in our own lives and in the lives of other brothers and sisters in our community.
- We will discern God's desires for our community communally— seeking God together in prayer, with open hearts."[14]

• Abbey Way (Minneapolis, Minnesota) •

Abbey Way Covenant Church is within the Evangelical Covenant Church of America.[15] With an emphasis on "shared spiritual practices and corporate rhythms versus programs or events, . . . more time is freed up to be together as a community of faith, sharing common life through meals, prayer, study, and play, while releasing people in mission within the context of their neighborhoods and workplaces." The people of Abbey Way "desire to create a way of living the Gospel life together that will sustain and nurture each person in and out of every season. . . . Placing a high value on each person's spiritual growth and ability to hear God, [they] endeavor to make space for wholistic interaction between both young and old, male and female, married and single as much as is appropriate and helpful for all."[16] The principles that undergird their practices consist in a will to be still, listening to God from a standpoint of commitment, and a willingness to change as they respond to what they have heard personally and collectively.[17]

Incarnational Ministries among the Poor

The second expression of Resurgent Monasticism consists of communities engaged in an incarnational ministry of "presence," serving the surrounding community by identifying with the poor, striving to improve access to quality education and health and hospice care, and supporting people at risk in society through such things as activity centers for young adults and shelters for abused women. They offer hospitality as basic to their understanding of mission, and they are primarily concerned with going deep in their explorations of the implications of discipleship for urban living, rather than on reaching out beyond their immediate neighborhood.

Many traditional monastic orders have for centuries dedicated their work to the service of the poor. The New Monasticism continues in this tradition, while embracing a wider constituency of members of their orders. They have no distinctive dress and welcome entire families, including the children, into membership. Some share a common living space, while others live apart but share in regular community meal and devotional times. Such communities express their commitment to work among the poor by establishing themselves in the poorest districts of urban conurbations. Groups of this sort have proliferated in recent decades.

• Servants (Vancouver, Canada) •

As part of the global ministry of Servants International, Servants Vancouver is "playing a part in seeing God's Kingdom come amongst our urban poor neighbours in the Downtown Eastside, Vancouver." They live as "an intentional Christian community, practising radical hospitality and sharing [their] lives and the love of Jesus in simple and practical ways with the surrounding community, hand in hand with a local church that shares the same vision." The people of Servants Vancouver are more concerned with building relationships with neighbors than with what they call "service delivery."[18]

• Reba Place Fellowship (Chicago, Illinois) •

Reba Place Fellowship, which was established in 1957, is, in its own words, "an intentional Christian community in Evanston and Chicago, Illinois. We are followers of Jesus Christ, freely sharing life and resources with one another and with our neighbors in order to demonstrate God's peace and justice in the world."[19] The members belong to the Mennonite tradition, and the community is closely linked to local Mennonite churches. While some forms of the New Monasticism consist of groups sharing accommodations and a common purse, this is not always the case.

• LivingStone Monastery (Newport News, Virginia) •

LivingStone Monastery, according to its Web site, "opened in February 2004 and is the former home of the Sisters of Poor Clare—a cloistered community of Franciscan nuns who lived there for over 50 years. Now a monastery in the Evangelical Tradition, LivingStone is a religious community called to support the local church, practice hospitality and create an environment for spiritual formation." LivingStone's approach is community based and holistic. It is also ecumenical, recognizing that individual congregations cannot exist in isolation, as this description attests: "LivingStone is a ministry of Hope Community Church and exists on the campus of Mosaic, a multi-congregational partnership of churches."[20]

Their idea is simple:

> one house, one God, many churches, shared resources. In our committed effort to keep to the monastic tradition, LivingStone is indeed still a house. In addition to housing six churches, LivingStone is a living community, home to 15 "workers" (some single, some married) who have committed this season of their lives to live and serve in LivingStone's calling. LivingStone's name was inspired by 1 Peter 2:4: "As you come to Him, the living stone—rejected by men but chosen by God and precious to Him—you also, like living stones, are being built into a spiritual house to be a holy priesthood, offering spiritual sacrifices acceptable to God through Jesus Christ."

Their range of ministries includes, among others, spiritual formation, recovery groups, and caring for individuals and families in difficulties by providing meals.

• New Jerusalem (Philadelphia, Pennsylvania) •

New Jerusalem is a residential addiction recovery community. Their neighborhood, on the west side of North Philadelphia, is an area with acute social problems, as evidenced by the fact that nearly 50 percent of the population suffers from drug or alcohol addiction. New Jerusalem describes itself as "a non-denominational spiritual community, focused on the principles of nonviolence, simplicity, and cooperative living." But their involvement stretches beyond their local context. "We understand addiction as one part of a vast network of social injustices that are particularly profound in the 'urban desert' of North Philadelphia. We are therefore deeply engaged with local, national, and international struggles for peace and justice."[21]

Other small intentional communities operate with a similar aim, including Nehemiah Community in Springfield, Massachusetts.[22]

Birthing "Fresh Expressions" of Church

The third expression of Resurgent Monasticism consists of monastic orders committed to the advance of the gospel in areas of the world and among peoples beyond the reach of the ministries of local churches. These mission orders attract a younger group of Christians and are a response to the growing realization that the church urgently needs not just younger leaders, but a different kind of leader. The church needs visionary, risk-takers who do not look to institutional churches to provide their financial security or career opportunities. They are prepared to venture into the unknown not as isolated individuals, but as cohorts that belong to a wider dispersed community. They do not undertake lengthy periods of training *for* mission, but are trained *in* mission. Recognizing that most failure in church leadership occurs through failure of character rather than competence, their training focuses on becoming biblically literate and on internalizing the spiritual disciplines.

• The Order of Mission (Sheffield, England) •

The Order of Mission (TOM), a group with which I am personally connected through my role as one of three "visitors" (i.e., consultants), was birthed in the joint Anglican and Baptist church located in Sheffield, in the parish of Crookes. The Anglican St. Thomas'

Church has had a fascinating history, with a reputation as a strong biblical teaching ministry that attracts many students, as well as serving its surrounding neighborhood. Both churches were profoundly influenced by the charismatic movement, and by the visit of John Wimber to the renewal conference held in Sheffield in 1987. Originally two separate congregations, they came together as a "Local Ecumenical Project" and have continued to be enriched by each other's traditions and to share their resources in order to address the needs of the city and reach out to younger generations. In response to its vision for the city of Sheffield, which has a church attendance rate that is estimated at 3.5 percent, the church has developed a model of dispersed cluster groups of mid-sized communities that use its LifeShapes approach (discussed in the previous chapter) as the "operating system" or toolkit by which to shape lives according to the teaching of Jesus. LifeShapes is not a "program," they say, because the principles taught must be continually revisited in the light of life's challenges and fresh insight gained through putting the principles into practice.[23]

The local impact of St. Thomas' ministries in reaching out to the younger generation received the recognition of the wider church, leading to the official formation of The Order of Mission on April 6, 2003, with the Archbishop of York and the Bishop of Sheffield leading the inauguration ceremony. Since then TOM has attracted approximately three hundred members. TOM describes itself as "a global community of pioneering leaders who follow Jesus." Under God, the members commit themselves "to each other for the purpose of taking the good news of Jesus to the nations."[24] Their goal is to make disciples who will in turn make disciples, and to initiate or participate in the birthing of new faith communities. They are equally concerned for the renewal of existing churches, stimulating them to catch that same vision. They seek to mount a determined challenge to the pervasive influence of consumerism, individualism, and religious pluralism, in which so many Christian churches find themselves increasingly marginalized and impotent.

The Order of Mission stands in the stream of movements in past centuries that responded to the spiritual needs of their day, such as the Celtic monks and nuns who first evangelized Ireland, Scotland, northern England, Scandinavia, and northern Germany. They did this by organizing themselves into itinerant bands that settled and formed communities alongside pagan settlements. By so doing, they were able to demonstrate the impact of the gospel in their own personal and corporate lives. In more modern times, the Methodists in eighteenth-century England and the Salvation Army in the nineteenth century also stepped outside the structures of the established churches, reaching out to the segments of the populations that they were failing to influence for the gospel. TOM also draws insight and inspiration from, and has established cooperative relationships with, mission agencies that forward the global mission of the church. Prior to its formation, TOM leaders such as Mike Breen and others consulted with a number of the traditional monastic orders both to learn from their long and rich experience and to seek to avoid as many pitfalls as possible.

Some members of the order are establishing new faith communities, including one family that serves and leads a network of missional congregations across the city of Bristol, with the approval of the Anglican bishop of the Bristol diocese. Their vision is "to see creative Jesus communities engaging and reaching out to every person and area of Bristol and beyond, so God's presence fills the city and it reclaims its great spiritual heritage, and lives into God's blessing in the 21st century."[25] Other members of the order, such as a group working in Århus, Denmark, are developing a design company that incorporates "kingdom principles" and helping those engaged in that high pressure industry to survive and thrive as followers of Jesus who strive to implement the life skills of disciples into their personal and professional lives.[26] Wherever they are located, and whatever their calling, members of TOM seek to influence the context in which God has placed them—whether urban, suburban, or rural; in developed or developing countries; in business, education, the arts, health care, social services, public or private sector, family or church. In their various callings members commit to intentionally reaching out with the gospel of Jesus Christ to those who do not know him.

TOM members are located all over the world. They are "spread throughout the UK with larger hubs in Sheffield and Bristol. There are TOM members throughout Europe based in Denmark, Finland,

Sweden, France, Germany, Slovakia and Italy. There are TOM communities in various states in the United States, across Australia and New Zealand and there are a small number of TOM members based throughout Asia and Africa."[27] Wherever possible, order members gather in "huddles" for accountability and support, with an annual weekend gathering that was held in Sheffield for the first few years of TOM's existence, including celebration, teaching, and the reception of new members into the order, but that has since been decentralized in various countries in response to the worldwide growth of the order.

TOM members have adopted and interpreted the traditional monastic vows into a contemporary context, committing themselves to a life of simplicity, purity, and accountability. The practical application of these vows is developed through the use of LifeShapes, with its intentional cultivation of the spiritual disciplines of listening to God, prayer, a rhythm of life expressed in rest and work, and a balance incorporating worship, discipleship, and witness. Unlike traditional mission orders, TOM members are people from all walks of life who are affirmed in their unique calling, recognizing that missional leaders are pioneers in their particular field, beyond simply being leaders in the church.

The Church of England has come to recognize that it needs to develop support and accountability structures that will better facilitate fresh expressions such as TOM. Consequently, it is has now established guidelines for the setting up of Bishops' Mission Orders within the dioceses of England.[28] These are early days, and it is still too soon to predict how many dioceses will take advantage of these new missional initiatives.

• Proposed Mission Order for North America •

In the North American context, David Fitch has proposed the formation of an order of mission called the Missional Order of St. Fiacre (the patron saint of gardeners!). His vision is for an order that will be sent out to cultivate Christian communities as gardens—places of spiritual cultivation, as distinct from grocery stores—in the cities, neighborhoods, towns, and villages of North America. They would establish communities "committed to a lifestyle of simplicity, frugality and bi-ministerial/bi-vocationalism to survive financially for the long term, yet be wise and prudent so as not to find themselves in hock or otherwise financially enslaved later on in life." Their specific commitments include "Scripture reading, prayer, corporate silence, mutual submission of one's emotions to God, mutual confession of sin, repentance and reconciliation, working out one's struggles, pains and joys as part of God's work in you for His Mission and finally a mutual benediction being sent into the Mission." Their essential structure to facilitate such a comprehensive commitment is a regular meeting in "triads" (groups of three).[29]

It will be interesting to see how much interest Dr. Fitch's proposal generates in the coming months. I am also aware of other mission orders in the process of formation in Canada and elsewhere. Time alone will tell just how significant these initiatives prove to be for the renewal of the church and the birthing of new faith communities.

Evangelical Agencies

Historically, the evangelical tradition has had a strong commitment to social engagement, in recognition that the gospel relates to the whole person and to the forming of faith communities that will have a transformative influence on society at large. However, during the last century this emphasis fell into neglect in some quarters, largely due to the controversy that raged, starting in the 1920s, over concerns of a perceived "sellout" to the Social Gospel advocates. The Salvation Army was one body that refused to succumb to this dichotomy, but in so doing it has struggled to maintain the balance between its evangelistic and social mandates.

From the beginning of the 1970s, increasing pressures within the evangelical constituencies insisted that such a dichotomy was unbiblical. The gospel could not be reduced to a message that was preoccupied with the individual's eternal salvation while still embracing God's broader agenda for the establishment of his reign here on earth. The church was seen as an anticipation and servant of God's wider purpose. A renewed commitment to social engagement was increasingly evident in a number of agencies that worked in the areas of evangelization and discipleship and viewed the former as an invitation to the latter, with discipleship essentially consisting of learning to become a faithful follower of Christ in today's society.

A number of evangelical agencies sprang up at that time, including World Vision,[30] which was founded in the United States in 1950 and grew to become a large international agency, and Tearfund (originally an acronym for The Evangelical Alliance Relief Fund),[31] which was founded in the United Kingdom in 1968. These agencies are involved in disaster relief, long-term community development projects addressing hunger and health issues, fair trade (which, in the case of Tearfund, happens through its subsidiary Tearcraft),[32] AIDS prevention and treatment, a concern for the global repercussions of climate change, especially on the poorer nations, and child sponsorship opportunities. While these agencies cannot be identified with Resurgent Monasticism, they have provided a climate of sacrificial service and global awareness.

• InterVarsity Christian Fellowship •

InterVarsity Christian Fellowship runs a program called Mission Year that offers college graduates opportunities to work with the poor in American cities. More specifically, Mission Year describes itself as "a year long urban ministry program focused on Christian service and discipleship. We take teams of young people, place them in an area of need, and help them to serve people and create community. We are committed to the command of Jesus to 'love God and love people,' by placing the needs of our neighbors first and developing committed disciples of Christ with a heart for the poor."[33]

• InnerCHANGE •

InnerCHANGE is a ministry within Church Resource Ministries that was inspired by the Franciscan Order and began in 1983. John Hayes, the founder of InnerCHANGE, emphasizes ministry *among* the poor and not simply *to* the poor. InnerCHANGE seeks to realize its calling to be missionary, prophetic, and contemplative.[34] Their key biblical text is from Micah 6:8: "what does the Lord require of you but to do justice, and to love kindness, and to walk humbly with your God?" (NRSV).

InnerCHANGE is comprised of "communities of missionaries living in poor, marginalized neighborhoods around the world— places most people want to avoid or ignore. We seek to live out the good news of Jesus among the poor, both with words and deeds."[35] They recognize that identification with the poor will entail change taking place within themselves, as well as within those among whom they minister. InnerCHANGE works in Asia in addition to being in the inner cities of Los Angeles, Minneapolis, San Francisco, and London.

Summary

Resurgent Monasticism takes many forms, as we have sought to illustrate in the course of this chapter. The churches in the West are in need of continuing renewal. The distinctive contribution of Resurgent Monasticism is to draw attention to the radical and all-encompassing nature of this renewal. It will not be achieved by focusing attention on one aspect of the church's life, leaving unexamined all other areas. It must comprehensively embrace the church's structure, worship, commitment to discipleship, and spiritual disciplines, and must ensure that local congregations and their dispersed faith communities become places of hospitality and outreach. In other words, the referral we are referring to entails the morphing of the church.

The history of monasticism bears witness to the incarnational mission of the church, representing a self-sacrificing servant spirit undertaken in an attitude of freedom and joy in the gospel. That history has also created valuable resources, such as that provided by the Rule of St. Benedict—but these resources need to be reinterpreted to apply to conditions in the twenty-first century. In addition, there are warnings to be learned from the past; for example, during the Middle Ages monasteries became both insular and wealthy, leading to their disillusionment at the time of the Reformation. The history of monasticism also indicates ways by which faith communities can be multiplied at low cost and with high impact, as clusters of believers establish an order of life, coupled with a commitment to sharing that life with the surrounding community. They witness to the power of the gospel of Christ by their personal and corporate living as signs of his coming reign on earth.

— 7 —

expanding networks

The appearance of a growing number of independent church plant-ing initiatives represents a further strand in the morphing of the church. Whereas some of these new churches are stand-alone ex-amples, others are centers of, or nodes within, new networks of faith communities. These emerging networks are both expanding and multiplying. We must first, however, distinguish between genuinely new networks and those that consist mainly of formerly independent churches that are now seeking greater significance by association with a family of churches. In this chapter, our focus will be on those networks that represent the birthing of new congregations and faith communities.

If the first test of the significance of a new network is to ascertain to what extent the churches are new and not simply pre-existent congregations that have transferred in, the second test is to ask where the people have come from who make up the congregations identifying with these networks. If they consist primarily of church-goers who have transferred their allegiance from churches they previously attended, these networks have simply contributed to the continuing fragmentation of the existing churchgoing population. As the Pew Forum research cited in chapter 3 reminds us, there is a great deal of movement between Protestant churches, as well as a significant movement of former Roman Catholics, who are often non-practicing members of the folk Catholic community. The new networks are only missionally significant to the extent that they are reaching out to people who have either given up on church, never been regular adult church attendees, or had no previous contact with a local church.

Historical Background

The origin of new networks can be traced back to the Jesus People revival of the 1960s, which gave birth to the Calvary Chapel movement and to the house church movement in the United Kingdom in the 1970s. The first Calvary Chapel in Costa Mesa, California, was opened in 1965 under the leadership of Chuck Smith, who continued as a leading figure in the Jesus movement.[1] Their rapid growth was fueled by conversions among the hippie culture, rather than through transfers from other churches. It is estimated that within a two-year period in the 1970s they performed well over eight thousand baptisms and were instrumental in twenty thousand conversions to Christ. To date the church has established 1,330 affiliate chapels across the world (with 22 in the United Kingdom). With the membership of the Costa Mesa church now reaching twenty thousand, it is one of the ten largest churches in North America.

The growth of the house church movement in the United Kingdom proceeded at a much slower pace, in a less responsive spiritual climate. Entrepreneurial leaders who traveled among house churches developed networks that wanted to follow their leadership, so they provided an apostolic or "covering" ministry designed to provide accountability and safeguards through external oversight. When we look back to previous centuries, beginning soon after the Reformation, we see that many of the independent denominations that either splintered from state churches or set up in protest were also founded by entrepreneurial visionaries.

Apostolic Calling

Traditional denominations are inhibited by an absence of such entrepreneurial leadership; or, to put it in biblical categories, they give little
room and encouragement to the apostle and the evangelist. Their dominant leadership models are that of pastor-teacher and administrator.
The problem with using the term "apostle" in many church traditions
today is that it is open to misunderstanding and misrepresentation.
The concern arises from the confusion of identifying the term "apostle"
with the twelve disciples of Jesus, who were apostles-in-training, and
represented a unique group. They were the foundational pillars of the
new people of God, corresponding to the twelve tribes of Israel in
the Old Testament.[2] For Luke, the author of his Gospel and Acts, the
apostles refer to the twelve. Professor C. K. Barrett writes,

> Historically, Luke's anxiety to represent the church in its mission
> to the world as the outcome of, and as continuous with, Jesus and
> his mission to Israel, leads him to tie down the notion of apostle-
> ship to the group of twelve whom he could describe as having been
> close disciples and companions of Jesus during his ministry, and to
> represent these twelve as responsible through Peter, for initiating
> the Gentile mission.[3]

The one exception is Luke's reference to Barnabas and Paul as apostles
in Acts 14:14. Martin Garner, in his brief but substantive study on
apostles for today writes,

> Luke is the one who amalgamates the original phrase "The Twelve"
> with the "apostles." It seems likely that he did this to counter part of
> the Gnostic challenge. The word *apostolos* had a contemporaneous
> use in Gnostic circles. In later years it became necessary to establish
> Jesus' true apostles, meaning those uniquely blessed as being eye-
> witnesses to the life, teaching and resurrection of Jesus, versus false
> Gnostic apostles. Luke's us of *apostolos* happened later than Paul's
> use of the word.[4]

In contrast to Luke, when Paul speaks of apostles, it is *never* with
reference to the Twelve. He is using the term in a different sense, not

as apostles of Christ, but as apostles of the church—a much wider group, who were the groundbreakers for the advance of the gospel and the planting of churches. Paul uses the term in this sense thirty-four times in his letters, while Luke, in Acts, uses the same term twenty-seven times, but almost always in reference to the Twelve. One exception is his reference to Barnabas and Paul as apostles in Acts 14:14. In fact, Paul identifies a number of apostles by name: Barnabas, Silas, Timothy, James the Lord's brother, Apollos, Junias (or Junia—a female apostle?),[5] Andronicus, Epaphroditus, and also includes himself in this wider company, and not as one of the Twelve.[6]

Martin Garner argues that if Paul's was the original use of the term "apostle," we should not allow the more restrictive understanding to become the normative definition. Garner, who himself exercises an apostolic ministry within the ranks of the Church Army in the Church of England, describes the role of the apostle in sharp distinction from the way in which it is used today by a number of self-proclaimed apostles. These individuals are people with supercharged egos who give themselves the title in order to enhance their standing as celebrity pastors of megachurches, or as leaders of a religious franchise. Garner challenges these misconceptions by emphasizing,

Apostles are perfectly made by God to do what only they can do.
- They are made for adventure, for taking risks, hardship and adversity;
- They are made for tackling the impossible;
- They have eyes of faith for the mission task in a way that leaders of [the] local church do not . . .
    . . . for talking to complete strangers;
    . . . starting from scratch with no resources;
    . . . tackling fear and prejudice;
    . . . communicating the good news to those who seem hardest to reach;
    . . . living without financial security.
All this is food for apostles, because they are made by God to do that. Though this all seems like hardship to the rest of us, ultimately it is fulfillment for the apostle. One problem for

apostles is that those around them often do not have the same "eyes of faith."[7]

Martin Garner's profile closely matches many of the individuals I have met, or been in touch with, in the course of researching the preceding chapters. They are individuals with deep passion and unswerving commitment to their apostolic calling. They are committed to the tasks of leading people to Christ and birthing faith communities among people that institutional Christianity is failing to reach. But this strong vision is coupled with personal humility, which arises out of their dependence on the Lord, as they attempt what can only be achieved by God-given guidance, strength, and resources. This humility also stems from the realization that they are vulnerable human beings on a steep learning curve.

In the endeavors of these individuals to establish and provide resources for networks of emerging churches, they often have to make it up as they go along, much like the early church. They will admit that they are learning more from their failures than from their successes. Peer mentoring plays an important part in their ongoing education, which is why they are frequent bloggers and value every opportunity to meet with others who bring insight based on experience.

In my own experience, they also welcome conversations with older leaders with whom they can share their vision, discuss the challenges they are facing, and receive counsel. The apostolic calling is a lonely one, but their independent spirit should not result in isolation, and needs to be tempered by accountability. Entering into situations where evil predominates means that they must believe that God can do the exceptional to achieve the extraordinary. Challenging the powers of darkness also entails suffering and persecution. But apostles, among whom Paul is a prime example, are given the strength and resolve to persevere against all odds (2 Cor. 11:16–33; Phil. 3:10).

In this chapter we will center our interest particularly on the new networks that have emerged during the past two decades. These networks circumvent the hierarchical control that is typical of denominational church planting initiatives.

Spreading Networks

The following examples represent a sample of new networks of churches that are beginning to make a significant contribution to the overall task of church planting among the spiritually disenfranchised and ecclesially disconnected.

• Association of Vineyard Churches •

The Association of Vineyard Churches began as a home-based, Bible study group in Southern California. John Wimber joined this group in 1982, and from that original group sprang a growing fellowship of churches that has spread to many parts of the world and is known for its emphasis on the empowering of God's people for ministry, with a special emphasis on healing and deliverance. Its influence spread beyond its ranks through the conferences led by Wimber, which attracted church leaders from many traditions, including mainline denominations. It was especially influential in the United Kingdom, where its impact continues to this day.

The movement stalled for a time, after Wimber's death in 1997, but has since recovered a sense of cohesive identity and its commitment to sharing the Good News, serving the community, and church planting. The Vineyard Association makes a significant contribution to contemporary worship music, with its songs adopted by many churches, including many that don't identify with the Vineyard's distinctive theological emphases.

Birthed in the Southern California subculture, many Vineyard churches continue to reflect a laid-back style and gentle, devotional worship ethos. In contrast, there are also Vineyard churches in urban settings that are more hard-edged in their lyrics and music and more boisterous in their worship expression. They also embrace a commitment to sacrificial, humble service in the communities where they are located. Their philosophy is to represent the "radical middle" of empowered evangelicals. Church planting remains a high priority, as evidenced by the resources the movement supplies and its high-quality newsletter, "Leading Edge." Today there are over 1,500 Vineyard churches worldwide.[8]

The Vineyard Association has also strengthened its inter-church relationships through the leadership it is giving to the more radical emergent church initiatives in the United Kingdom. This leadership is coming through the work of people like Jason Clark, pastor of Vineyard Church Sutton in London, who also serves as national coordinator for Emergent UK, the network of emergent churches.[9] Vineyard Music International also provides a common ground where music like that of the Burn Band, a group that originated from the Burn Church, an alternative service at the Vineyard Church of St. Albans, can bring people together around a shared interest. The Burn Band is "on the forefront of modern UK Vineyard worship. They released 'Beautiful' in 2002, which has sold over 45,000 copies worldwide and just this year 'All from you' which has received critical acclaim. . . . The Burn Band, led by Samuel Lane, [brings] a new passion, energy and intimacy that is rarely seen in worship music today."[10] The Vineyard Association continues to be a vibrant and growing movement. Although birthed in a suburban Southern California context, many of the churches have assumed more radical worship styles as they have engaged urban culture and responded to social needs. Their influence is more widespread in Europe and elsewhere among traditions other than those that are predominant in the United States.

• Newfrontiers •

The Newfrontiers movement, which originated in southeast England, began with the vision of Terry Virgo in 1968. It now consists of over six hundred churches and has spread to over fifty countries. "With a passionate commitment to build the church according to New Testament principles, [Newfrontiers believes] that the most effective form of evangelism is worked out from strong local churches. Churches where each member participates, the gifts of the Spirit are outworked, where there is joy in caring one for the other, where there is a desire to make a difference in society and to reach those in need. [Newfrontiers aims] to achieve this by restoring the church, making disciples, training leaders, planting churches and reaching the nations.[11]

• Church Multiplication Associates •

Church Multiplication Associates (CMA), led by Neil Cole, exists "to support and encourage church multiplication movements by developing new resources focused on reproducing disciples, leaders, churches and movements from the place where [they're] planted and finishing at the ends of the earth."[12] More precisely, it is a voluntary association of expanding networks of simple churches working together to learn from each other in living out the mission of Jesus. Its structure is intentionally fluid, recognizing that an organic system will both root and reproduce in different ways. At the local level, CMA's "Greenhouse" provides "a relational context for leaders from a city or region to gather together in a supportive environment and learn more about church and church planting from one another and the Scriptures."[13] Regional weekend retreats and regular monthly gatherings provide the foundation on which this facet of CMA's mission is based. Greenhouse sites can be found throughout the US and around the world.

Church Multiplication Associates originated with the Grace Brethren Fellowship of Churches, beginning in 1990 with a group of pastors in the Southern California/Arizona District. Churches from many denominations are now represented in the Association. They identify with CMA's shared vision to link with "a growing and emerging family of churches intent on being alive with Jesus, mutually encouraging and spontaneously reproductive."[14] Neil Cole has worked in close association with church planting consultant Bob Logan. Together they co-authored *Raising Leaders for the Harvest* in 1995. After a slow start, a breakthrough came in 1998 when Neil and "a small team began Awakening Chapel in Long Beach, CA by reaching out relationally to lost urban post-moderns in a local coffeehouse."[15]

> Within months many were coming to Christ and so a second church was commissioned under the leadership of Rob Ferris. Doug Lee came on board with a call to start a cell-celebration church in Fontana, California. We were not only seeing fruit and reproduction, but also learning key concepts for establishing a church multiplication movement. By the end of 1999, there were nine Awakening Cha-

pel churches started. Awakening Chapels has continued to multiply across the globe due to interns from around the world spreading this movement.[16]

A significant feature of Church Multiplication Associates is its realization of exponential growth at every level: in terms of new Christians reaching out to their friendship circles and beyond; with new churches giving birth to other faith communities; and with networks generating new networks of churches. Their approach is organic rather than engineered, which resulted in impressive growth during their first six years of operation.

> In our first year, we began ten new churches. In our second year, Church Multiplication Associates (CMA) started 18 churches. The next year, we added 52 new starts. The momentum was beyond our expectations. In 2002, we averaged two churches a week being started and had 106 starts. The following year, we saw around 200 starts in a single year. We estimate that close to 400 churches were started in 2004, but counting the churches has become a daunting task. At the time of this writing [2005], there have been close to 800 churches started in thirty-two states and twenty-three nations around the world, in only six years.[17]

Neil Cole understands the dynamic of networks in developing the concept of the organic or simple church.

> The organic or simple church, more than any other, is best prepared to saturate a region because it is informal, relational, and mobile. Because it is not financially encumbered with overhead costs and is easily planted in a variety of settings, it also reproduces faster and spreads further. Organic church can be a decentralized approach to a region, nation, or people group and is not heavily dependent upon trained clergy.[18]

They recognize that churches are reproducible when the converts are the workers, and when leadership is developed from among them. Training leaders on the apprenticeship model results in individuals who know their context because they were nurtured within it and because their training has not removed them from that context.

When leaders are trained on a traditional academic model, they often become so changed in the process that many find it difficult to return to the environment in which they were nurtured. Furthermore, their former friends and social networks regard them as no longer belonging. If leaders are going to influence those networks, then it makes no sense for them to break contact with those networks by sending the leader-in-training elsewhere for an extended period.

• The Ecclesia Network •

Ecclesia is another US-based network that describes itself as "a relational network of churches, leaders, and movements that seek to equip, partner, and multiply missional churches and movements."[19] Although this network was only two years old at the time of writing it had already planted eight churches around North America. Ecclesia identifies its collective mission as one of "revolutionizing the church in order to reach our post-Christian culture."

Typical of many Generation X and Generation Y Christians, Ecclesia combines concerns for and involvement in both their local neighborhoods and other continents. They also express a common theme that they are a community of people who have not arrived spiritually but rather are on a faith journey "traveling the uncertain path of ministry together."[20] In response to this adventure of faith, with all its uncertainty, Ecclesia represents a network of churches that "support one another in the process of establishing imaginative gospel communities both locally and globally."[21] They provide opportunities to share resources and ideas through seminars and provide congregational coaching and assessment.

Ecclesia's vision is to form a network, not of existing churches seeking to affiliate for the sake of a stronger identity and significance, but of new churches, with each one appropriate to its context. They also endeavor to work across denominations "aligning churches based on a common mission" and are committed to the renewal of declining churches by providing "an empowering environment." In all aspects of their message and mission they seek to be rooted in Scripture and to learn from the experience of the church across the centuries. One of their churches has developed a teaching series for a class called

"Epic," which is designed to draw their community more fully into God's story. Churches within the Ecclesia network fully embrace the past while "engaging with the realities of the future," and they stand with Christians everywhere in embracing the Apostles' and Nicene Creeds as "foundational for how we understand and express the truth of God's story today." Deep roots in Christian tradition are important to them, something they see as setting them apart from the Boomer "now" generation, but their attitude is one of *learning from* the past, not *living in* the past. This attitude helps explain why their worship emphases are both sacramental and creative in their expressions and why they do not shy away from cultural engagement, which ultimately is a reflection of their missional identity.

Such is their vision, but it is no "pipe dream" without substance. Ecclesia provides church planting boot camps, leadership gatherings, and theological forums. Within their growing network are churches in Blacksburg and Richmond, Virginia; Feasterville, Pennsylvania; Odenton, Maryland; and Hollywood and Santa Monica, California. Kairos Los Angeles was birthed in September 2004 and is now meeting in a community center in Santa Monica. When Kairos West LA was birthed in November 2006, Kairos Los Angeles became Kairos Hollywood, and the name "Kairos Los Angeles" came to signify the overarching organization.

Kairos Hollywood sees itself as "gathering a variety of wounded people together, crying out to our Creator to breathe new life into us. Through this new life we desire to see broken communities become communities of faith and see God's kingdom come to earth neighborhood by neighborhood." Although a young church, it already has a wider vision, with several members of the community involved in taking medical care to the poorest parts of Tijuana, Mexico, through Healing Hearts, while others work with the Solis Foundation serving the poor and visiting orphanages. The Solis Foundation was founded by J. R. Woodward, pastor of Kairos Hollywood, with the help of a businessman in his congregation.

But their wider involvement is not at the expense of their local commitment. Members of their church community have started volunteering at non-profit organizations such as Chrysalis, Ocean Park Community Center, Mathnasium, Pico Youth and Family Center, and the Westside Pregnancy Resource Center. They further engage their culture through softball, book clubs, moms' clubs, dance classes, and hockey. Many of their initiatives arise through the five "canvas" groups into which their small community is divided. Members of these canvas groups have undertaken to serve their local communities in a variety of ways, including preparing backpacks for low-income students in the public schools; hosting a Christmas party for those with nowhere to celebrate the holiday; and, with the help of others in Santa Monica, serving a regular barbecue to the homeless in the city.

Although still a young church, Kairos Hollywood released a group of its members to begin the West Los Angeles church. Following in Kairos Hollywood's footsteps, the people of Kairos West LA have also been active in the community, including becoming involved in the East Hollywood Neighborhood Council, to the extent that their pastor has even been invited to serve on the newly formed council. They are active in neighborhood projects, including hosting a series of concerts in public venues.[22] A new ministry called "Artist @ the Fountain" invites people to serve the neighborhood by fostering an appreciation for art and artists while also marshalling resources for social justice causes such as The Unembraced, a ministry to orphans in Kenya. Such a breathtaking range of activities demonstrates that a small church, when it is not preoccupied with buildings and programs, can create a climate in which ministry initiatives take place. They release their members, who see their primary calling as serving the broader community. Ministry is not confined to the church premises or restricted to the members, but occurs on the streets.

Ecclesia, in its mission to turn churches from consumerism to service, is attempting something that is revolutionary for the churches of North America. The radical nature of its vision is perhaps most clearly exemplified in the results of a survey conducted a number of years ago by Win Arn, a leader in the early years of the church growth movement in North America. The survey revealed that 89 percent of members of nearly one thousand churches believed that the church existed "to take care of my family's and my needs," while only 11 percent said that it existed to win the world to Christ.[23] This self-focus continues to present one of the greatest challenges to church leaders committed to moving their congregations from maintenance to mission.

One of the founding churches of the Ecclesia network is New Life Campus Fellowship, a multicongregational church of approximately one thousand people that reaches out to university students at Virginia Tech and in Radford, as well as a growing number of community members in the New River Valley. They see their ministry within a college town as strategic for their call to send members elsewhere—kingdom people planting new churches. Although they are a large congregation, they measure their success by their *sending* capacity and not their *seating* capacity!

Multisite Churches

As churches become more technologically savvy, they have been able to develop the multisite church model—that is, a church that meets in multiple locations, linked by satellite and video. Individual churches are part of a larger network that gives them access to conferences and Web sites where the multisite church model is further explained.[24]

The multisite church movement began in earnest in the 1990s but has really taken off in the past eight years, with current estimates of about 2,000 multisite churches in the United States. According to Todd Rhoades of Monday Morning Insight, an October 2005 multisite church conference released statistics regarding growth in the number of US churches operating as multisite: In 1990, there were ten multisite churches. In 1998, that number had expanded to about a hundred. And in late 2005, there were more than 1,500 multisite churches in the United States.[25]

In most cases, multisite churches have pastoral oversight at each site, conducting worship services with live bands and their own worship and prayer leaders. But for the sermon they patch in to the mother campus via satellite or video. This mix enables them to retain a degree of local ownership and contextualization, while still benefiting from association with the mother church and other off-site venues.

• North Coast Church (Vista, California) •

North Coast Church of Vista, California, was one of the first churches to use video technology to create an off-site campus. The decision to create a "Video Café" that would use a combination of live worship and a video feed of the message was driven by a consideration of available space, in addition to concerns about the time and funding that would be required for the construction of a new facility. Today North Coast Church has four different campuses, including both live and video worship venues, with over 6,500 in attendance on an average weekend.[26]

• Fellowship Church (Dallas/Fort Worth, Texas) •

Fellowship Church, pastored by Ed Young, describes itself as one dynamic church meeting in five locations: Grapevine, Plano, downtown Dallas, and Fort Worth, Texas; and Miami, Florida.[27] The church's ministry focus is to provide real answers to people concerned about "finances, relationships, parenting, careers," and so forth.[28] Their welcome extends to people of all backgrounds, both families and singles. The Grapevine church, located in the Dallas-Fort Worth metro area, describes itself as "a community of people led by Christ to bring hope, strength and change to the world—one life at a time."[29]

• Seacoast Church (Georgia and South Carolina) •

Some churches, such as Seacoast Church in Georgia, have adopted the multisite approach as an alternative to enlarging their campus when they reach a point of having outgrown their current facilities, opting instead for a more decentralized approach. Seacoast Church maxed out when the congregation reached three thousand in 2002. Today the church meets in nine locations distributed throughout Georgia and North and South Carolina.[30]

• Bethlehem Baptist Church (Minneapolis, Minnesota) •

Bethlehem Baptist Church, pastored by John Piper, is another example of a church that has moved to a multicampus church in order to facilitate further growth. In addition to their original downtown campus, they now have two additional sites in Mounds View and Burnsville, covering the northern and southern sides of the city.[31]

> Typically, the pastor bringing the sermon preaches at the evening Saturday service at the Downtown Campus and the message is digitally recorded. On Sunday morning, the preacher for the weekend preaches on rotation at one of our three locations. On the other two locations, a digital recording of the Saturday evening message is replayed for Sunday morning worship services. The only aspect of the worship service that is delivered by recording is the sermon.[32]

• Mars Hill Church (Seattle, Washington) •

Mars Hill Church was founded in 1996 with a small group meeting in the home of pastor Mark Driscoll and his wife Grace. For the next seven years, Mars Hill met in various locations throughout the city until, in 2003, the church's one thousand attendees moved into a renovated hardware store. Within three years they had outgrown that facility, so in early 2006 they became a multicampus church meeting in three different locations to accommodate their nearly six thousand attendees. Mark's sermons are recorded and shown at each of these locations.[33]

• Redeemer Presbyterian Church (New York, New York) •

Redeemer Presbyterian Church, which began in 1989, is a dynamic congregation in the heart of Manhattan. Pastored by Dr. Timothy Keller, Redeemer has nine affiliate congregations.[34] It demonstrates its commitment to church planting through its Church Planting Center, which has a vision "to ignite and fuel a city-focused, gospel-centered, values-driven church planting movement in New York, in cooperation with the wider Christian church, and to assist national leaders and denominations to plant resource churches in the global centers of the world."[35] In partnership with Mark Driscoll's Acts 29 network, which "exists to start churches that plant churches," Redeemer organizes an annual church planting conference.[36]

From the outset, their intention was to spark a movement with a vision to facilitate new church planting throughout New York City, with churches that inherit the vision and values of the mother church. While their primary calling is to reach the young professionals who are disconnected from the church, they are also trying to meet the social needs of those who are impoverished, homeless, and addicted through substance abuse. They are particularly interested in planting churches in neighborhoods that are committed to Christian community development and the rebuilding of devastated communities. Their approach as a church is a holistic one, as they seek to help Christians relate their faith to their professional life and to their engagement with the arts. Everything is based on small groups, in which individuals learn in relationships and are nurtured in their faith.

Concerns Related to Multisite Churches

The multisite model also raises some legitimate concerns. By bringing in the celebrity speaker via satellite or video, it places the other churches in the community at a disadvantage. It is like Walmart moving into town, with its access to resources not available to the smaller neighborhood stores. Consequently, the overall impact of the local branch of the multisite model must be assessed in relation to the combined witness of the churches serving the area. Another issue to be taken into account is the impact a star performer has on the recognition and nurturing of those within the congregation who are called by God to communicate the full counsel of God. Does the use of a video link acknowledge and inspire these gifts, or does it frustrate and disempower local leadership potential? A final concern related to multisite churches is whether the proclamation of the same message to multiple locations will hinder the church's ability to address specific issues at each individual site. At the very least, local leaders need to make sure they are providing specific application at the conclusion of the message.

Virtual Church through Internet Campuses

A new frontier for multisite churches is to go into cyberspace with an Internet campus. An Internet campus typically enhances a live streaming video of a worship service with interactive elements that allow viewers to do things like chat with each other, respond to polls, and submit prayer requests.[37] Flamingo Church is one example, with Pastor Brian Vasil reporting 1,300 PC connections weekly.[38] Visual Studio Web site provides a wide range of technical assistance, including streaming video, lobby chats (to facilitate online conversations between members), instant messaging, a campus pastor, prayer teams, push technology (allowing the sending of information and the opportunity to respond to questions), and much more.[39]

This model gives rise to some serious theological concerns: Can disciples be made without interaction in a face-to-face community? How can mutual accountability be exercised when it is possible to hide behind an electronic mask? Is so-called virtual church a sellout to individualism and the breakdown of authentic relationships?

Network Catalysts

Apart from the emerging church and missional church networks, a number of other organizations and groups are stimulating the development of new networks. Some organizations come alongside leaders of networks to provide counsel, disseminate information, and facilitate peer-group consultations. Others are less directly involved, providing opportunities for celebration, inspiration, and instruction through large-scale national events that have a widespread appeal.

• Leadership Network •

Leadership Network has committed considerable resources to stimulate church planting initiatives both across North America and in Europe. It recognizes that churches need to think beyond the methods they have relied on in the past, believing that "God is calling churches to radically rethink their passion and strategies for harvesting the unchurched and penetrating lostness." They are convinced that there is no one method or model that will be adequate for the challenge; rather, "there are multiple means for starting churches." The belief that "if we build it they will come" may work to fill a sports stadium, but church planting can no longer be undertaken on that basis. Faith communities need to be birthed within each cultural context, whether that consists of cowboys, bikers, skaters, hip-hop fans, or the homeless.[40]

Leadership Network is committed to assisting the morphing of churches by instilling a church planting DNA into the new churches, reclaiming declining churches for new church beginnings, and still some traditional church plants. "Since 1984, the DNA of Leadership Network has been the diffusion of innovation in the Church. Of the estimated 350,000 churches in North America, a small number are recognized as 'islands of health and strength,' and exhibit significant influence on the other churches by introducing innovative and breakthrough ideas. These innovators and early adopters are the client base for Leadership Network."[41]

Leadership Network has identified at least four characteristics of the churches that are having a significant impact on the church planting movement:

- These churches have started new churches within the past five years.
- Church planting is a priority of the church, with a goal to start multiple congregations.
- They have a kingdom mindset.
- They are innovators in church planting.

Three years into the project, Leadership Network reported, "the Church Planting cohort of fifteen churches has produced 321 new church plants involving over 31,000 people."[42] Their ministry extends beyond the transitioning of existing churches to organizations that engage in church planting initiatives by means of organizing Church Planting Leadership Communities. They are facilitating the development of collaborative relationships and networks with innovative church leaders.

Leadership Network has released a comprehensive study of the state of church planting within the United States.[43] Headed by Ed Stetzer, the director of Lifeway Christian Resources, this extensive study among forty-five church planting networks estimates that approximately four thousand new churches are established per year in the United States, which is perhaps an all-time high, reflecting a significant increase over estimates from previous years. Another significant finding in the report is the degree of cooperation and sharing of resources that is evident among church planters, with numerous training tools offered free of charge online and the promotion of national church growth conferences. In 2007, Houston, Texas, hosted a citywide church planting conference called "Accelerate" that attracted 150 local church planters.

A third observation noted in the report is one that we have also identified in previous chapters, namely that the initiative in planting churches is coming more from local churches and networks than from denominations. While many church plants are denominationally *connected*, they are not denominationally *controlled*. The new churches are themselves becoming reproducing churches.[44] But this does not mean identifying one model to apply in every situation. Rather, each situation will give birth to models that are appropriate for that context.

• Stadia, Churches of Christ •

Stadia is a church planting facilitating agency arising from the Church of Christ that assists in starting new churches across the United States.[45] They approach this vision by championing collaborative church planting networks, including partnerships with existing church planting associations and churches. It is not Stadia's intent to assume the responsibilities or take the place of existing church planting associations or agencies, but to come alongside those entities when invited.

For groups that are exploring the possibility of church planting, Stadia is able to recommend organizations that can provide assessment tools, coaching, and training in church planting and the financial aspects of the task. Their choice of name reflects their commitment to the planting of new churches: "We chose the word Stadia as our name because we believe the size of Heaven will be measured by the number of souls that are there, and because we believe that planting new churches is the most effective method for winning the lost."[46]

Stadia does not work independently, but through grassroots church planting networks that typically consist of "four or more church/organizations, which have come together to plant a new church."[47] It is these networks that work together to identify and support leaders by providing ongoing mentoring and financial resources. By partnering with these grassroots initiatives they are able to draw upon a wider knowledge and network of church planting agencies.

• Acts 29 •

Acts 29 is the church planting network that grew out of Mars Hill Church in Seattle. Acts 29 recruits and supports church planters across the United States, in addition to reaching out to other areas of the world. Currently the Acts 29 network includes forty-five churches in the western United States, twenty-seven in the central region, and thirty-three in the eastern region. Acts 29 supports the church planter through "boot camps" and other training events held around the country and the world.[48]

A Resurgent Reformed Movement

Christianity Today alerted its readers to the resurgent Reformed phenomenon in September 2006 with its lead article by Collin Hansen, "Young, Restless, Reformed."[49] In that same year the movement, demonstrating serious theological engagement, expressing enthusiasm, and with a strong appeal among younger leaders, held a conference in the Minneapolis Convention Center that attracted 3,100 participants. The theme for the conference was "Above All Earthly Powers: The Supremacy of Christ in a Postmodern World," and the principal speakers were David Wells, Don Carson, Tim Keller, Mark Driscoll, Voddie Baucham, and John Piper.[50]

When I visited the Web site of the conference I was struck by the charismatic expressiveness of the worship, which did not fit my stereotype of serious looking Calvinists! One of the groups represented at the conference was the Sovereign Grace network of churches that combines charismatic worship and gift expression with Reformed doctrine![51] In 2008, Mars Hill Church in Seattle, pastored by Mark Driscoll, is also promoting preaching and church planting, hosting conferences under the auspices of Resurgence and Acts 29. The appeal of this resurgent Calvinism has spread beyond its traditional power base in the historic Reformed churches of Europe to include many Southern Baptists, largely through the leadership of R. Albert Mohler Jr., president of The Southern Baptist Theological Seminary in Louisville, Kentucky.

• Sovereign Grace Ministries •

C. J. Mahaney began a series of charismatic meetings in the early 1970s with Larry Tomczak in the Washington DC area. In 1982 they founded The People of Destiny International, which was renamed "Sovereign Grace Ministries" in 2003. The movement represents an unusual combination of charismatic worship and understanding of ministry with Reformed theology, in that they believe in the continuance of the ministry gifts of apostles and prophets for today.

Sovereign Grace Ministries "is a family of churches passionate about the gospel of Jesus Christ. We are devoted to planting and supporting local churches, with a strong doctrinal basis that is evangelical, Reformed, and charismatic."[52] Currently there are over sixty affiliate churches located in twenty-four states.[53] In the United States, forty-two of their sixty-four churches represent church plants, as distinct from existing churches that have affiliated with their movement. Sovereign Grace offers specialized training for church planters, emphasizing the development of godly character and providing academic training and practical resources to guide in team formation, raising financial support, and apostolic oversight.

• Spring Harvest •

The United Kingdom provides two significant examples of large-scale conferences that have a nationwide impact across a wide spectrum of denominations and that appeal to churchgoers of all ages. Such nationwide gatherings are much more difficult to organize and unlikely to have the same impact in the United States, due to the size of the country and the self-contained nature of the many denominations, networks, and independent churches that make up North American evangelicalism.

Spring Harvest has been running annual weeklong family camps in the United Kingdom since 1979.[54] Currently, gatherings are held in two locations: Skegness on the east coast and Minehead on the southwest coast. Each site has chalet accommodations for about ten thousand, and together they register a total attendance throughout the year of more than forty-five thousand. Each year the major theme is explored through a multitude of workshops and seminars that participants have the opportunity to choose from. There are also a variety of worship styles to suit different traditions and ages. On returning to their churches, enthusiastic groups take with them the worship they have experienced, the songs they have learned, and the teaching from which they have benefited.

• New Wine •

Another significant initiative arising out of the influence of John Wimber in the United Kingdom is New Wine. This began as a Christian festival in 1989, led by Anglican bishop David Pytches and his colleague Reverend Barry Kissell who, at that time, were leading St. Andrew's Church, Chorleywood. Its conferences, consisting of celebrative worship and Bible teaching, have added impetus to the charismatic movement, drawing together churches nationwide with three summer conferences that attract over thirty thousand delegates each year. New Wine has maintained its Anglican leadership through John Coles, with two London churches providing an organizational base: St. Barnabas', Finchley and St. Paul's, Ealing. New Wine works in close collaboration with Soul Survivor, a networking youth initiative led by Mike Pilavachi, and also holds conferences in the United States and New Zealand.[55]

Summary

New networks are bringing fresh waves of energy to church planting, utilizing a range of innovative strategies. They are also identifying a

new generation of leaders who are not just young leaders but represent a different kind of leadership. They are "apostolic"-type leaders
in the sense of being groundbreakers who exercise inspiring faith
and personal sacrifice. They often operate with minimal financial
resources or institutional backing and are moved and sustained by
a strong sense of God's call. They gather other leaders around them
and are prepared to live a day at a time, making it up as they go
along, with the resilience to survive setbacks.

We have drawn attention to the distinction between networks
that represent new growth and networks that simply consist of
previously independent churches joining a franchise. Some of
these networks arise out of or are contained within a broader
and older tradition. In these respects they are in reality "fresh
expressions" of church, a notion with which we began the survey
in this book.

Leaders of new networks must recognize the tendency to develop their own traditions and procedures over time, so that they
in turn become increasingly institutionalized. There is no escaping
this development, which is why the church must always be in a
state of continuous renewal. While organizational structures are
necessary, they must function to *facilitate* rather than to *frustrate*
the mission of the church. Structures are supportive skeletons,
not restrictive corsets! Many younger leaders are eager to find
older leaders to serve as their mentors, providing the wisdom of
experience as well as the caution that can only come from battle
scars received in the course of conflict, as a result of battles lost
and won.

The emergence of new movements is a sign that the Lord has not
given up on the church. The examples provided in this chapter give
a sense of the wide range of traditions represented by new church
planting networks. As the church fulfills its functions as the body
and bride of Christ it will always be the "becoming church," giving
birth to new forms of church, as well as revitalizing churches that
have long histories or have become captive to the limited perspectives
of their own contemporary culture. "New" does not always signify
the latest or most recent. More often, it describes that which is fresh
and vigorous, whatever its life stage.

8

the heartbeat of worship

In this final chapter we will look at the contribution of the alternative worship movement (often called "Alt.Worship"), which does not represent a distinctive stream as such, but rather reflects a reassessment of the ways in which we worship, and its impact on our understanding of the nature of the church, especially in Western contexts. It is a stream that has its own source but that mingles with the other streams described in previous chapters. Its transcendent worship emphasis challenges the modernist notion that we humans can renew the church through our own strategic thinking and technical expertise. And its stress on creative participation challenges the twin heresies of consumerism and individualism that are so prevalent in our culture.

A spate of new songs of worship has accompanied every significant period of renewal within the church. In addition to drawing upon the rich heritage of hymnody from previous centuries, each new generation must find the forms of expression that enable it to worship the Lord in ways that are appropriate in its time and place.

It represents not only a rediscovery of ancient forms that speak in fresh ways to our generation but also a passion for creative embrace of the arts to couple truth with impact.[1]

In assessing the numerical strength of the alternative worship movement, I believe it would be a mistake to regard it as a sideline, because its influence is far wider than its numbers. Though its beginnings were in the United Kingdom, it is now attracting increasing interest here in the United States. Alt.Worship groups are springing up across North America. In 2008 a media team of students from Calvin College, led by Professor Kevin Corcoran, spent seventeen days in London visiting alternative worship groups and attending a conference with many of their leaders. The Archbishop of Canterbury, Rowan Williams, who is a strong supporter of "fresh expressions" of church, was one of the plenary speakers.[2]

Among the leading names associated with Alt.Worship in the United Kingdom are Pete Rollins of Ikon in Belfast; Kester Brewin of Vaux, Jonny Baker of Grace, Dave Tomlinson of Soul Space, all from central London; and Jason Clark from the Sutton Vineyard. Most of these are featured in the book on emerging churches that I coauthored with Ryan Bolger.[3]

Alternative Worship

The alternative worship movement seeks to relate the gospel to a segment of the population profoundly influenced by the culture of postmodernity. This is far more pervasive than those who are intellectually committed to postmodernism as a philosophical position. Many people have embraced its tenets through the embedded assumptions of popular culture, without necessarily realizing where they have come from. It is a mistake to think that this phenomenon is confined to the post-Boomer generations; in reality, it is more a psychographic than a demographic grouping and is characterized, at least in part, by a rejection of any overarching story (metanarrative) or, more accurately, by a profound suspicion of those who seek to impose *their* metanarrative. The search for identity and significance goes beyond the individual's story or even the story of the group to which they belong.

In such a climate, worship services provide participants an opportunity to listen and learn from one another, believing that our understanding of the nature of God, and of the gospel made known through Jesus Christ, is bigger than our ability to grasp. This leads to attitudes of tolerance and humility, and to the recognition that the theologies we construct are all tentative, due to our human limitations, resulting in much ambiguity and mystery in matters of faith. Changing contexts raise new questions. They are committed to *biblical* theology, while being suspicious of *systematic* theology. Professor Corcoran comments, "They believe that God is bigger than any theology and that God is first and foremost a story-teller, not a dispenser of theological doctrine and factoids. Theology for them, therefore, is conceived as an ongoing and provisional conversation."[4] Consequently they tend to be theologically pluralistic, bringing together leaders from diverse backgrounds—from Reformed to Pentecostal, from liturgical to those more at home with spontaneous expressions of worship.

They place greater emphasis on right living than on right believing, out of their conviction that we will be judged by our orthopraxis rather than our orthodoxy—that is, what we *show* we believe rather than what we *say* we believe. The mental framework is more *centered* set than *bounded* set, more concerned with the direction in which people are moving than whether they are "inside" or "outside" a doctrinal barrier. Many are concerned to birth faith communities that not only reach out but also reflect the culture in which they are embedded. Steve Collins, a leader within the Alt.Worship movement, made the point in 2005 that theirs is a faith expression within culture, not within a parallel "Christian" culture.[5] In missiological jargon this represents "contextualization."

However, in taking this stand, leaders must recognize that the relationship between gospel and culture is complex. A naive contextualization results in baptizing the culture wholesale, whereas a critical contextualization adopts a more discerning approach, distinguishing those elements in the culture that evidence the affirming and redemptive presence of God from those that are a denial of the values of the reign of God inaugurated by Jesus. It also raises the question, "Can one have a community of the kingdom without those within it submitting to the reign of the King?"

Communities That Relate to the Broader Culture

The call to obedience to the radical message of Jesus leads to the formation of communities that interface and intermingle with the broader community. Their vision is to become a transformative presence. They are prepared to accept the fact that you cannot have mission without mess, because the church itself consists of forgiven sinners and not perfected saints, and that those to whom they offer hospitality will come with their own cultural baggage and unresolved issues. Theirs is a dispersed community that lives amid the rough-and-tumble of everyday life, so a premium is placed on togetherness, on journeying with and alongside others. Reflecting on his recent London visit, Professor Corcoran provides the following assessment from his Reformed perspective:

> I believe that there is much to praise and get excited about in altworship/emerging expressions of faith and practice. Indeed, for those in the Calvin community it is easy to hear in these emerging voices and stories echoes of the Kuyperian vision that animates Calvin College itself. But there are also places to pause and register concerns. For example, some in the emerging/altworship movements are allergic to creeds and the particularity of Christian beliefs, falsely (in my view) believing that finite human beings cannot say true things about an infinite God. Moreover, in their bid to be culturally relevant, there is the risk of unwittingly succumbing to the same sort of base consumerism that is the hallmark of this generation. There is also the risk of capitulating to the cult of hip and celebrity that is consumerism's offspring.[6]

Alternative worship must not be construed as an evangelistic strategy to make the Christian faith relevant to a particular generation or culturally defined group in order to appear "cool and fashionable." It is first and foremost the Christian community's expression of worship that identifies with its generation and social network.

They believe that their worship must express their celebration of the presence of the Lord within that broader culture. In other words, our worship should not convey the message that God only relates to past generations and alien cultures.

As a movement, Alt.Worship emerged in the United Kingdom in the 1980s and spread to the United States around the year 2000. In keeping with other streams of emergence, Alt.Worship spans many Christian traditions. Most groups are small, numbering under fifty, but with widespread influence through the exchange of worship ideas and resources.

Creative Participation

The Alt.Worship movement is in part a protest against consumerism and the importation of songs, many of them with trite and self-focused lyrics. Those who embrace Alt.Worship seek authenticity through faith expression that truly represents the people who make and take part in it. Worship entails creative participation. It is in the exploration of various themes—as individuals work together to generate ideas to express those themes, each person contributing their artistic gifts—that worship flows out of the corporate life of the faith community.

Creating worship events is not the preoccupation of a few, resulting in the marginalization of the bulk of the congregation. It is an activity in which each person is invited to contribute and is thereby validated, recognizing that everyone is made in the image of God and made to express the creativity that God has bestowed. So everyone is encouraged to participate at his or her own level of ability, which clearly entails a certain amount of toleration and affirmation, as well as an openness to the risk that is run by practicing inclusion to such an extent. Alt.Worship has an element of playfulness that welcomes the opportunity to learn from one's own (and the group's) mistakes and even to laugh together about them—and ultimately, not to take oneself too seriously. Every person's contributions toward particular elements are valued, and they are all brought together into a coherent presentation.

While it is highly creative, Alt.Worship draws upon ancient forms and liturgies without being bound to them. Steve Collins describes, for example, what *doesn't* happen in the context of Alt. Worship:

- sermons or didactic teaching
- sitting in one place all the time
- worship bands, choirs or organs
- one person at the front directing everything [though in some instances the worship is DJ led]
- PowerPoint presentations[7]

This last presupposition reminds me of an experience where I was co-teaching with a younger colleague. When I produced my Power-Point presentation he responded, "That's so nineties, Eddie!"

One thing that *does* happen within the context of Alt.Worship is attentiveness to the use of space. The configuration of furniture in a worship space says a great deal about the center of power and influence. Rows of seats arranged to face a stage, for instance, send the message that the platform is the scene of action. Alt.Worship instead emphasizes nondirectional space; the total area is the "happening place." People may be seated on the floor, on beanbag chairs, or on soft furnishings. Tables may be scattered around to provide meeting places for more intimate conversation, or to display elements with which worshipers can interact, known as "installations": candles to light, sand or water to sift through your fingers, pens and crayons to write or color with, clay to mold, and so forth. There may also be special places for personal prayer or for seeking the counsel of another person.

Ministry happens spontaneously in small groups and one-on-one within the context of corporate worship. Sometimes artists, such as potters or painters, will work on a piece during the worship time and will offer their finished work as a contribution to the worship theme of that worship service. Worship gatherings are also a time to express hospitality toward invited guests and those who have simply dropped in to check things out. Refreshments may be served, either during an interval or at the conclusion of the act of worship. Each individual worship gathering is unique, and Alt.Worship centers throughout the world, including those in the United Kingdom, Australia, Canada, Germany, New Zealand, and the United States, reflect the multifaceted nature of this movement.[8]

Alternative Worship and the Arts

A number of churches, festivals, and Web sites are promoting the arts within the life of Christian communities. Workshops are available to disseminate ideas and provide practical coaching.[9]

• Greenbelt Arts Festival (Cheltenham, England) •

Greenbelt describes itself as "an independent Christian charity working to express love, creativity and justice in the arts and contemporary culture in the light of the Christian gospel."[10] Since 1974 it has provided a meeting place and ongoing creative stimulus to alternative worship groups.[11] Over the years its scope has widened beyond the evangelical music subculture to include concerns for global justice and the environment. Today it meets at the Cheltenham Racecourse and draws a crowd of over seventeen thousand each year. It enjoys the collaboration of a wide range of Christian organizations that have "helped Greenbelters re-imagine the church as an infectious global conspiracy, working for God's peace, healing and friendship in previously unimagined ways."[12] In the last few years Greenbelt has gained a reputation for living on the edge, while at the same time celebrating the traditional worship forms. The Big Hymn Sing at the 2007 Greenbelt Festival was organized by BigFish, who ran a Web site inviting attendees to vote from a list of 114 hymns. The top ten great hymns of the church were sung at the Festival.

Greenbelt has extended its reach beyond the United Kingdom, serving as a gathering point for those who are experimenting around the world in new worship forms. For instance, Transmission, an alternative liturgical community in New York City that is led by Isaac Everett and Bowie Snodgrass, presented *Play Dress-Up!* at the New Forms Café at Greenbelt in 2006. *Play Dress-Up!* takes the idea of dressing up for church and for childhood games and invites participants to be transformed by vestments, textiles, and the power of imagination by Scripture passages such as the description of the priests' garments in Exodus 28; God clothed with splendor and majesty in Psalm 104; and the woman with the flow of blood touching the hem of Christ's garment in Matthew 9, Mark 5, and Luke 8. Since then, their community has been gathering on the first and third Wednesdays of each month. Each "transmission" includes a home-cooked meal, ritual, prayer, and time to be together.[13]

• Grace Ealing (West London, England) •

Grace Ealing provides a good example of a small group that has had a widespread influence. Referring to itself now as a "Christian alternative worship community/network,"[14] Grace began in St. Mary's Anglican church in 1993 by offering creative, participatory expressions of worship. The group has had its ups and downs during its relatively brief history, seldom numbering more than fifty participants and sometimes falling to single digits. But they have been amazingly creative in their worship expression, designing events to which they would be able to invite their friends, many of whom were from London's clubbing culture. Founded by Mike Starkey, the group is currently led by Jonny Baker.

Alternatives to Traditional Church

Some groups within the Alt.Worship scene seek to demonstrate an alternative to popular conceptions of church, which so often appear disconnected from wider society. They also represent communities that are supportive of the arts and express their worship by incorporating poetry, music, and the visual arts that represent the offerings of the community as an essential part of their dialogue with God. They embody the honest and welcome questions, aspirations, and frustrations of the seeker.

• Visions (York, England) •

St. Cuthbert's Church is in ancient city-center York and has a long-established tradition as a center for evangelism and charismatic worship in the Church of England. Since the renewal experienced in the 1970s, St. Cuthbert's has moved in more radical directions in response to the missional challenges presented by a post-Christendom culture. It now hosts Visions, which describes itself as "a church for people who don't like church."[15] In step with many evangelicals who now draw from a broader range of church traditions, they now represent a more eclectic approach.

> Many of us grew up in the evangelical tradition, and we affirm its sense of equality of access to God and its respect for the Bible, but we resist its frequent association with right-wing fundamentalism. Indeed, we accept a lot of the liberal analysis that social action against poverty, homelessness, and so on, is an important job of our society. However, we also have charismatic roots and believe that the move of the Spirit is one way of bringing healing and wholeness to people's lives. In some ways our approach to church services is very Catholic in terms of being sacramental and using ritual; it also draws on Orthodox traditions by using all the senses and rich visual symbols. On the other hand, our spirituality is not confined to services, and hence we adopt the Celtic view that all parts of our daily lives can be sacramentalized. This brings us partway along the road to Creation Spirituality (Matthew Fox), and the Spirit in Creation (Jürgen Moltmann). Some of our mystical roots are in Hildegarde of Bingen (1098–1179), Thomas Merton, and Julian of Norwich. No doubt I've forgotten to mention several other important influences. . . . Finally, a quote from St. Francis of Assisi: "Preach the Gospel at all times. If necessary, use words."[16]

In keeping with most other emerging churches, they provide seekers with a welcoming space in which they can express their doubts, fears, and messiness without risking rejection by so doing. The environment is one in which seekers need not feel embarrassed or reluctant to talk about Jesus, but more than that it provides a community in which his love can be experienced. The people of Visions recognize the importance of the arts in deepening their faith journey, incorporating the visual arts, dance music, and technology into their worship experience. The space in which they worship is "a very atmospheric old building," with some parts dating back to 687

AD. They self-identify with the alternative worship movement, making the tongue-in-cheek comment, "Lots of people are suspicious of organized religions: we'd be perfect for them since we're developing a model of disorganized religion!" They do not reject tradition, but rather mine it and recreate it within their setting.

> We are part of a movement rather loosely termed Alternative Worship, but the name doesn't really say enough—we mean that our response to the Divine Presence has to be born from our own experience together, as individuals and as a community, and not simply accepting whatever forms of worship are given to us. However, that is not to say we reject the past, rather that we see Christian traditions as a rich field of possible resource to draw on. But we also draw on contemporary culture in finding expression for our spirituality.[17]

They seek to avoid the limitation experienced by some alternative worship groups that tend to be self-centered in their focus. Visions is clear about its missional intention. "We don't wish to bury our heads in the sand. We want to connect with each other, God, and the hurting people around us. To support each other in a world where we can all feel a bit isolated sometimes."[18]

• Sanctus1 (Manchester, England) •

Sanctus1 seeks to exegete the city as it "gathers together to discover more about Christ, culture and community." It is located in the heart of the city, where so many younger adults gather, especially during the weekend for a "good time" in the clubs. The city center has a reputation as a place where binge drinking and unruly behavior are common. In this context Sanctus1 is a faith community "exploring God and spirituality within the city." Rather than seeking the safe haven of an ecclesiastical sub-culture, they seek to engage the broader culture, looking for the presence of God in one another and in expressions of popular culture in contemporary film, art, and music. They believe that "the dynamic nature of the city centre reflects the people that we are; a fluid organic community that believes that the creative spirit of God is active and moving in culture."[19]

Sanctus1 is sponsored by both the Anglican and the Methodist churches in the city and is part of the Fresh Expressions initiative that we described in a chapter 3. For a time they met in a variety of locations, but in 2005 the Methodist church opened Nexus as a unique space within the northern quarter of Manchester's city center. This has now become the primary meeting place for Sanctus1, while also operating as a café and a base for various projects within the city, including music and dance workshops for local artists and quarterly art exhibitions. Nexus also houses a recording studio.[20]

The people of Sanctus1 describe themselves as "an inclusive Christian community" who "believe that God is not defined by theology." They welcome dialogue between different theological positions, emphasizing that authentic dialogue "involves listening and real listening involves change." They are on a journey together, not knowing the outcome, but believing that they will encounter the presence of God along the way. "Our journey is one of exploration but fortunately it is a journey in which we have a guide that lights our path and walks beside us in times of blessing and of trouble."[21]

"Third-Space" Hospitality

Sociologists speak of "first-space," meaning family or inner circle of friends, and "second-space," where we work, and "third-space," where we socialize. In our fragmented urban societies people seek a safe third-space where they can make friends, exchange ideas and concerns, and relax in a congenial atmosphere. Many churches fail to provide such a context in which friendships can develop.

Within the alternative worship stream of emerging churches there is a growing café church network. Examples can be found in Sydney and Melbourne, Australia, as well as in the United Kingdom and North America.[22] The café atmosphere provides a welcoming environment in which all can contribute and benefit. It makes the church culturally accessible, especially to those who have had negative experiences of church in the past or who have had little or no contact with institutional religion and find traditional worship formats irrelevant to their daily life. As a stimulus and backdrop to the conversation, café churches sometimes host DJ nights and provide the opportunity for creative artists to share their talents, revealing spiritual insights and provoking questions. The seating arrangement means that conversation takes place naturally around the tables and circles of seats.

The alternative worship stream has done much to promote creativity and to explore themes that embrace the whole of life. It encourages full participation, which can lead to new depths of understanding as each group develops its ideas, and is enriched by mutual interaction. It seeks to replace passive consumerism with homegrown worship events that give expression to the gifts bestowed upon the local community of believers.

Morphing Worship to Embrace the Whole of Life

The fact that corporate worship not only includes each person but also embraces the whole of life is strongly emphasized in many of the psalms. Consequently, we do the psalms a disservice if we restrict contemporary psalm-based worship songs to a few triumphant, celebrative verses. Clearly there is much cause for celebration, as we recall and relive all that God has done in Christ on our behalf. But we also recognize that we live as part of creation, which is "groaning as in the pains of childbirth" (Rom. 8:22). We cannot escape the pain and anguish of a world that still awaits its full redemption. We live with unanswered questions and unrelieved pain and suffering.

If there is no place for such anguish in our worship, due to an exclusive emphasis on celebration, then our worship is liable to become escapist, representing our living in denial or delusion—that is, until we reach the point where we have to be honest with ourselves. There are painful times in life when words of triumph and praise that we mouth to God no longer find an echo in our hearts or shape the way in which we live our lives. The range of emotions expressed in the psalms, from ecstatic joy to crushing guilt, gives us permission to be open and honest with God. Our worship should embrace every human emotion. In uttering our cries of anguish we can experience a profound healing.

The psalms provided us with wonderful examples of a rich hymnody that embraces the whole of life with honesty and theological depth. They face the harsh realities of tough situations, including betrayal by friends, life-threatening illness, and anxiety-induced sleepless nights. Some psalms work through these experiences, testifying to answered prayers with the resolution of the issues, while other psalms end with the issues unresolved. Many psalms are deeply personal, while others speak to the great assembly of God's people and look beyond to the wider world. In the theology of the psalms, God is not reduced to the level of a tribal God but is proclaimed as the Lord of the whole earth. It celebrates the whole creation and acknowledges God's control over the forces of nature. God is indeed the Lord of the harvest.

John D. Witvliet, director of the Calvin Institute of Christian Worship, has provided a valuable resource exploring the significance of the psalms for Christian worship. He writes,

> The Psalms speak of both social justice and personal transformation; they embody hand-clapping exuberance and profound introspection; they express the prayers of both the exalted and the lowly; they are fully alive in the present, but always point to the future on the basis of the past; they highlight both the extravagance of grace and the joy of faithful obedience; they express a restless yearning for change and a profound gratitude for the inheritance of faith; they protest ritualism but embody the richest expression of ritual prayer.[23]

So many churches in the Western world underutilize the psalms, or ignore them entirely, to the impoverishment of their corporate worship. As Witvliet discerns, the language of the psalms helps us develop a wide range of essential speech habits in regard to our relationship with God. He writes, "*I love you. . . . I'm sorry. . . . Thank you. . . . Help. . . .* Words like these are the building blocks of healthy relationships."[24] He invites us to consider the fact that each of the 150 psalms expresses at least one essential communication habit, and states that praying the psalms is one of the best ways to "pray in the Spirit" (Eph. 6:18; Jude 1:20).[25]

Many of the psalms provide examples of dialogue with God, as the psalmists talk through issues, reminding God of past events as a basis for their urgent petitions. Furthermore, they offer a corrective to mind-numbingly repetitive references to the Almighty, by using a diverse range of metaphors, each of which addresses a different aspect of God's character. Witvliet identifies fifty-seven names that are used in the course of the psalms, which together provide a rich tapestry that both corresponds to and challenges our many needs and moods.[26]

A Universal Call to Worship

The psalms are not only comprehensive in their themes but are also extensive in the global scope of their vision. They see beyond the present worshiping community, calling upon the nations—and the whole of creation—to join them in worship. Many of the calls to worship in the psalms "ring with delight: trees clap their hands; whales and hippos sing praise, in which all creation is caught up in a symphony of shalom to God."[27]

The psalms further demonstrate the close tie between worship and witness, for the one flows naturally and inevitably into the other. Witness is represented as the overflow of our worship.

> Sing to the LORD a new song;
>   sing to the LORD, all the earth.
> Sing to the LORD, praise his name;
>   proclaim his salvation day after day.
> Declare his glory among the nations,
>   his marvelous deeds among all peoples.
> For all the gods of the nations are idols,
>   But the LORD made the heavens. (Psalm 96:1–5)[28]

It is ironic that there is such a strong awareness of "the nations" in many of the psalms even as this awareness is sadly lacking in most of our contemporary hymns. This significant omission may represent a loss of missional nerve and commitment in the post-colonial Western world. It is the churches of the Global South that have taken up the challenge of world evangelization in our day with the greatest enthusiasm.

Introspective, self-improvement Christianity falls far short of the intention of God for his creation. If our worship begins and ends with us, then it has been reduced to the level of spiritual self-indulgence. True worship draws us near to the heart of God and his love, which so loved the world that he gave his only Son for its salvation (John 3:16). Worship not only experiences the glory of God but does not rest until that glory fills the whole earth as the peoples of the world submit to his Lordship.

> The Lord reigns, let the earth be glad;
> Let the distant shores rejoice. (Psalm 97:1)

In scanning the psalms we find a number of interrelated themes that provide a powerful corrective to any tendency to domesticate worship and confine it to the narrow world of any worshiping community. The psalms reiterate the fact that the God we worship is no tribal deity, but the Lord of all creation. He is Lord above all gods. He is concerned with the destiny of nations and looks to the time when they will acknowledge him as Lord of lords. The temple in Jerusalem, in which the psalms were first sung, was not intended to serve simply as a national shrine, but as a house of prayer for all nations.[29]

Summary

In this concluding chapter we have affirmed that worship is the heartbeat of mission and that congregations need to be active participants, rather than passive consumers. The Alt.Worship movement provides theological insight as well as offering a stream of practical suggestions. Theologically, creativity in worship arises from the conviction that humans are made in the image of God and are thereby bestowed with a creative capacity to glorify their Creator in worship by offering back to God the fruits of a rich diversity of creative expression. Leaders in this movement rightly emphasize that the spotlight in congregational worship must not be directed toward a few gifted individuals, such that the bulk of the congregation is marginalized and left (often quite literally) in the dark. Ultimately, attention is directed toward God, rather than being celebrity-focused. The table and open space are the focal point of worship, rather than the podium and stage.

In order to translate the theory of full participation into practice, the Alt.Worship movement mostly finds its expression in smaller congregations, or in large churches that are subdivided into smaller units or mid-size communities. In large churches that do not have such a structure, participation in worship celebrations inevitably becomes representative rather than all-encompassing.

At their best, Alt.Worship services strike a chord with the surrounding community, because they are indigenous in style and address the current issues that resonate with the community. Offering fresh perspective and enabling people to see themselves more clearly, the challenges to their faith journey are honestly depicted and biblically informed in the context of worship, thereby providing new insights, stimulating faith, and injecting hope.

We have also cautioned that too restrictive a focus on creative participation within a small group context can result in worship becoming increasingly self-focused. The *heart* of worship must never be separated from the *legs* of mission. The psalms establish this link at a doxological level, but it remains for the church, empowered by the Spirit, to translate vision into commitment. Worship makes possible the joyful commitment to break through restrictive cultural barriers in order to take the good news of the universal reign of Jesus Christ to all the world.

conclusion

In reviewing what I have written, I am acutely aware that I have merely been scratching the surface. At the outset I admitted that *ChurchMorph* could not present a comprehensive picture of God's initiatives through his faithful people, but that it could only provide samples and a few illustrations. Yet, I trust that I have covered sufficient ground to give an impression of both the extent and the complexity of the missional movements taking place throughout the churches of the Western world.

I have restricted my coverage primarily to England and North America, but in so doing, I want to acknowledge the conversation and peer mentoring taking place among church planters throughout Europe. My friend Mike Breen, who is in touch with many of these developments, informs me that the networks of church planters with whom he is in contact have a shared goal of birthing 750 new faith communities.

Within this complex picture there are strident voices both within and outside the emerging and missional streams that can muddy the waters. Those who are part of the conversation must ensure that when offering critiques we speak *to* one another rather than *about* one another, for each side needs to listen to and learn from the other. Furthermore, we must refrain from dismissing the whole enterprise on account of the statements of a few individuals with whom we may strongly disagree. Bearing in mind that we are presenting a wide range of initiatives, nobody speaks on behalf of everyone, or even a significant segment.

In the midst of the current turbulence, we must keep in mind some fundamental convictions. First, we must engage with the big picture that unfolds in Scripture from Genesis to Revelation, recording a multifaceted, comprehensive account of God's redemptive engagement with humankind. We are all prone to edit the story, whether from a conservative or liberal standpoint, but we should take care not to let this edited version be the final word. Second, we must celebrate God's creation and ensure that we are responsible stewards of it. Third, we must seek to have hearts that are filled with the love of Jesus Christ, who lived among us as one of us, laid down his life on the cross for our salvation, and continues in heavenly intercession for the salvation of the world. Fourth, we must make the mission of Jesus the model and inspiration for our own ongoing mission, which he has entrusted to his church. Fifth, we must continue to love the church as the body and bride of Christ, striving for its continuing renewal and faithfulness in carrying out its God-given mission. Sixth, we must be humble and patient toward one another, as we each come with a limited understanding and compromised obedience. Finally, let us come in faith and hope, knowing that God's commitment to us as forgiven sinners is expressed in an everlasting covenant—and that the best is yet to come.

This book has not been about the destruction of the church, nor does it bewail its fragmentation. We have described it as the morphing of the church, as it reconfigures in response to the missional challenge of a post-Christendom Western world. Just as we celebrate God-inspired diversity in creation, so we acknowledge and learn to celebrate diversity that is evident in God's new creation. This would be a dull and disturbing world if everyone were like me! And there is so much more richness among the people of God than is evident even in the local church to which I belong.

This study has traced the surges taking place within the churches of the Western world. But we have yet to see whether these hopeful and inspiring initiatives result in a turning of the tide in church attendance and quality of discipleship—and even more significantly, whether the new configurations will birth new faith communities and revitalize existing ones to such a degree that they make a significant impact on the communities to which they belong and in which they serve. We have the assurance of Christ's promise, not just for the survival of the church, or even for its restoration, but for its upbuilding, even as it is still in the process of construction.

appendix

distinctive features of morphing churches

A number of helpful summaries have been written that identify the distinctive features of emerging missional churches. Here is a selection of those summaries that provides a comprehensive overview of their characteristics.

According to a working document developed as part of the Gospel and Our Culture Network's "Transforming Churches Towards Mission" project, the empirical indicators of a missional church are as follows:

1. The missional church proclaims the Gospel.
2. The missional church is a community where all members are involved in learning to become disciples of Jesus.
3. The Bible is normative in this church's life.
4. The church understands itself as different from the world because of its participation in the life, death, and resurrection of its Lord.
5. The church seeks to discern God's specific missional vocation for the entire community and for all of its members.
6. A missional community is indicated by how Christians behave toward one another.

7. It is a community that practices reconciliation.
8. People within the community hold themselves accountable to one another in love.
9. The church practices hospitality.
10. Worship is the central act by which the community celebrates with joy and thanksgiving both God's presence and God's promised future.
11. This community has a vital public witness.
12. There is a recognition that the church itself is an incomplete expression of the reign of God.[1]

Kester Brewin offers five characteristics of emergent systems (summarized below, followed by brief descriptions and illustrations).

1. They are open systems—as opposed to closed; "change-from-within"
2. They are adaptable—self-organized as dictated by local, not global, circumstances
3. They are learning systems—"sensing, learning, adapting, and changing"; self-renewing
4. They have distributed knowledge—"no key leader . . . is seen as the fount of all knowledge" (e.g., the Internet); pursuit of truth is a shared experience (e.g., Microsoft—"closed truth" model; Linux—"open source" approach)
5. They model servant leadership—role of leaders, according to Keith Morrison, is to "change the perceptions of a situation," rather than simply to "announce change"[2]

Ryan Bolger and I have identified three core practices of the emerging church, along with six outcomes of these practices.

Three Core Practices:
1. Identify with the life of Jesus—orthopraxis; simplicity; engagement
   • From reading Jesus through Paul to reading Paul through Jesus

- The reign of Christ has been inaugurated
- The Spirit has been outpoured
- The Gospels lead to the Cross; they do not begin with the Cross

2. Transform secular space—social justice and community rejuvenation
   - From invitation to engagement
   - Holistic spirituality—challenging the sacred/secular divide
   - Life-embracing spirituality
   - Finding God in popular culture (Barry Taylor)

3. Live as community—you don't *go* to church; you *are* the church
   - Redefining the meaning of "church": family, people, decentralized
   - From casual and contractual to covenantal
   - Anticipatory signs of the reign of God

Six Outcomes:

1. Welcome the stranger—inclusion with a view to transformation
   - The inclusive practices of Jesus—a place at the table
   - Evangelism is a way of life, not an event

2. Serve with generosity—social justice and community involvement
   - Challenging the consumer culture of exchange
   - The kingdom comes as gift, and often as surprise

3. Participating as producers—from consumers to contributors
   - Providing opportunities for each person to contribute their story
   - Encouraging interactivity and dialogue

4. Create as created beings—each according to their gifts and passion
   - Creativity is participating in God
   - Includes all ages
   - Consists in bringing what one already has
   - Involves lighthearted playfulness

5. Lead as a body—"situational leadership" (John Adair)
   - From stifling control to creative freedom
   - Mike Breen's guiding principles:
     - Lightweight and low maintenance
     - Low control and high accountability
6. Merging ancient and contemporary spiritualities—draws upon the early church fathers, Celtic spirituality, medieval mystics
   - Eclectic spirituality, drawing from many Christian practices, both ancient and modern
   - Corporate spirituality, involving listening and responding[3]

Tom Sine offers the following "characteristics that are common to many different emergent expressions," which I have summarized as follows:

1. Little interest in the propositional, dogmatic approach to theology
2. Committed to creating innovative ways to engage in one particular cultural context
3. Tend to be highly experimental and artistic, often working compellingly with image and word
4. Tend to offer multilayered, experimental worship that draws on both ancient symbols and images from "profane" culture
5. Call people to an authentic, embodied, whole-life approach to faith
6. Outwardly focused on mission, not only to engage a specific group, but with a desire to have an impact on the lives of people in their communities and the larger world
7. Concerned with a broad range of social issues, including justice, reconciliation, and creation care[4]

Tony Jones, the national coordinator of Emergent Village, provides the most comprehensive list of characteristics, which he describes as "Dispatches from the Emergent Frontier" in his scholarly treatment, *The New Christians.*

1. "Emergents find little importance in the discrete differences between the various flavors of Christianity. Instead, they practice a generous orthodoxy that appreciates the contribution of all Christian movements" (p. 8).
2. "Emergents reject the politics of left versus right. Seeing both sides as a remnant of modernity, they look forward to a more complex reality" (p. 20).
3. "The gospel is like lava: no matter how much crust has formed over it, it will always find a weak point and burst through" (p. 36).
4. "The emergent phenomenon began in the late 1990s when a group of Christian leaders began a conversation about how postmodernism was affecting the faith" (p. 41).
5. "The emergent movement is not exclusively North American; it is growing around the globe" (p. 52).
6. "Emergents see God's activity in all aspects of culture and reject the sacred-secular divide" (p. 75).
7. "Emergents believe that an envelope of friendship and reconciliation must surround all debates about doctrine and dogma" (p. 78).
8. "Emergents find the biblical call to community more compelling than the democratic call to individual rights. The challenge lies in being faithful to both ideals" (p. 81).
9. "The emergent movement is robustly theological; the conviction is that theology and practice are inextricably related, and each invariably informs the other" (p. 105).
10. "Emergents believe that theology is local, conversational, and temporary. To be faithful to the theological giants of the past, emergents endeavor to continue their theological dialogue" (p. 111).
11. "Emergents believe that awareness of our relative position—to God, to one another, and to history—breeds biblical humility, not relativistic apathy" (p. 115).
12. "Emergents embrace the whole Bible, the glory and the pathos" (p. 144).
13. "Emergents believe that truth, like God, cannot be definitively articulated by finite human beings" (p. 152).

14. "Emergents embrace paradox, especially those that are core components of the Christian story" (p. 163).
15. "Emergents hold to a hope-filled eschatology: it was good news when Jesus came the first time, and it will be good news when he returns" (p. 176).
16. "Emergents believe that church should function more like an open-source network and less like a hierarchy or a bureaucracy" (p. 180).
17. "Emergents start new churches to save their own faith, not necessarily as an outreach strategy" (p. 197).
18. "Emergents firmly hold that God's Spirit—not their own efforts—is responsible for good in the world. The human task is to cooperate with God in what God is already doing" (p. 202).
19. "Emergents downplay—or outright reject—the difference between clergy and laity" (p. 204).
20. "Emergents believe that church should be just as beautiful and messy as life" (p. 213).[5]

notes

Chapter 1 Megatrends Convulsing the Western World

1. See David T. Olson, *The American Church in Crisis* (Grand Rapids: Zondervan, 2008), for a comprehensive study of membership and attendance trends. See also the "U.S. Religious Landscape Survey," conducted by the Pew Forum on Religion and Public Life, http://religions.pewforum.org/. Exceptions to the general picture of decline are the growth of some more conservative and smaller denominations, megachurches, and new networks.

2. David Kinnaman and Gabe Lyons, *un-Christian: What a New Generation Really Thinks about Christianity . . . and Why It Matters* (Grand Rapids: Baker, 2007), 25.

3. Ibid., 28.

4. The Kinnaman/Lyons research on the issue of involvement in politics clearly represents young people's awareness of the conservative voice within evangelicalism and their lack of knowledge of the books and blogs emanating from the "evangelical left," represented by Jim Wallis, Tony Campolo, Ron Sider, Gary Haugen, and others.

5. Kinnaman and Lyons, *unChristian*, 33.

6. Collin Hansen, *Young, Restless, and Reformed: A Journalist's Journey with the New Calvinists* (Wheaton, IL: Crossway, 2008).

7. See Barbara Johnson, *The Critical Difference* (Baltimore, MD: Johns Hopkins University Press, 1980); and J. A. Cuddon, *A Dictionary of Literary Terms and Literary Theory*, 3rd ed. (London: Blackwell, 1991).

8. Gordon D. Fee, *Philippians* (Downers Grove, IL: InterVarsity, 1999), 93.

9. See Peter Senge et al., *The Necessary Revolution: How Individuals and Organizations Are Working Together to Create a Sustainable World* (New York: Doubleday, 2008).

10. Christian Smith, "Getting a Life: The Challenge of Emerging Adulthood," *Books and Culture*, November/December 2007, 10–13.

11. Ibid., 11 (emphasis original).

12. Mark Kelly, "Study: Fewer Young People Attending SBC," Baptist Press, http://baptistpress.com/BPnews.asp?ID=27143 (accessed October 7, 2008).

13. Trevin Wax, "Bridging the Generation Gap in the Southern Baptist Convention," http://trevinwax.com/2008/01/07/bridging-the-generation-gap-in-the-sbc/.

Chapter 2 Post-Christendom Churches

1. George R. Hunsberger and Craig Van Gelder, eds., *Church between Gospel and Culture: The Emerging Mission in North America* (Grand Rapids: Eerdmans, 1994); Darrell L. Guder, ed., *Missional Church: A Vision for the Sending of the Church in North America* (Grand Rapids: Eerdmans, 1998); George R. Hunsberger, *Bearing the Witness of the Spirit: Lesslie Newbigin's Theology of Cultural Plurality* (Grand Rapids: Eerdmans, 1996); Craig

Van Gelder, ed., *Confident Witness, Changing World: Rediscovering the Gospel in North America* (Grand Rapids: Eerdmans, 1999); Darrell L. Guder, *The Continuing Conversion of the Church* (Grand Rapids: Eerdmans, 2000); James V. Brownson, Inagrace T. Dietterich, Barry A. Harvey, and Charles C. West, *StormFront: The Good News of God* (Grand Rapids: Eerdmans, 2003); Lois Y. Barrett, *Treasures in Clay Jars: Patterns in Missional Faithfulness* (Grand Rapids: Eerdmans, 2004).

2. Guder, *Missional Church*, 2.

3. Alan J. Roxburgh, *The Sky Is Falling* (Eagle, ID: ACI, 2005), 12 (emphasis original).

4. Alan Hirsch, *The Forgotten Ways* (Grand Rapids: Brazos, 2006), 274.

5. Ibid., 24–25.

6. Alan Hirsch, "Missional the New Emergent?" The Forgotten Ways: The Missional Musings of Alan Hirsch, http://www.thefor gottenways.org/blog/2008/06/23/missional -the-new-emergent-not-on-my-shift/ (accessed August 17, 2008).

7. John Drane, "Looking for Maturity in the Emerging Church," originally delivered as a lecture at Manchester Cathedral, May 2007, available as a PDF at http://2churchmice .files.wordpress.com/2008/12/maturity-in -emerging church2.pdf.

8. Ori Brafman and Rod A. Beckstrom, *The Starfish and the Spider: The Unstoppable Power of Leaderless Organizations* (New York: Portfolio/Penguin, 2006).

9. Sara Savage and Eolene Boyd-MacMillan, *The Human Face of Church* (Norwich, UK: Canterbury, 2007), 4.

10. Ibid., 11.

11. Doug Pagitt, comment posted on Emerging Pensees, http://emergingpensees .blogspot.com/2006/10/converging-church .html.

12. Kester Brewin, *Signs of Emergence* (Grand Rapids: Baker, 2007), 35 (emphasis original).

13. Scot McKnight, "Five Streams of the Emerging Church," *Christianity Today*, February 2007, 36, http://www.ctlibrary.com/ ct/2007/february/11.35.html (accessed October 14, 2008). As McKnight points out, Andrew Jones is known on the Internet as "Tall Skinny Kiwi" (http://tallskinnykiwi.org).

14. Alan Hirsch also speaks of the emerging missional church in *Forgotten Ways*, 66–72.

15. Kester Brewin, comment posted under "2008 Will Be About . . . ," http://kester.type pad.com/signs/2008/01/2008-will-be-ab .html.

16. See D. A. Carson, *Becoming Conversant with the Emerging Church* (Grand Rapids: Zondervan, 2005); Roger Oakland, *Faith Undone: The Emerging Church—A New Reformation or an End-time Deception* (Silverton, OR: Lighthouse Trails, 2007); and Ted Kluck and Kevin DeYoung, *Why We're Not Emergent, by Two Guys Who Should Be* (Chicago: Moody, 2008).

17. Barry Taylor, *Entertainment Theology: New-Edge Spirituality in a Digital Democracy* (Grand Rapids: Baker Academic, 2008), 146.

18. Hunsberger and Van Gelder, *Church between Gospel and Culture*, 289–90.

19. The Gospel and Our Culture Network, "Empirical Indicators of a 'Missional Church,'" *The Gospel and Our Culture* 10, no. 3 (September 1998): 7, http://www.gocn.org/ newsletters/pdf/103-newsletter.pdf (accessed November 14, 2008).

20. Ibid., 6.

21. C. E. B. Cranfield, *Romans: A Shorter Commentary* (Grand Rapids: Eerdmans, 1985), 328.

22. See Bob Hopkins and Mike Breen, *Clusters: Creative Mid-sized Missional Communities* (3 Dimension Ministries, 2007), downloadable PDF available at www.3dministries .com.

23. See, for example, Taylor, *Entertainment Theology*.

24. Harlan Cleveland, *Nobody in Charge* (San Francisco: Jossey-Bass, 2002), 44.

25. Tom Sine, *The New Conspirators* (Downers Grove, IL: InterVarsity, 2008), 39.

26. For a fuller discussion of the impact of the culture of the information age on

leadership in the church, see Eddie Gibbs, *LeadershipNext* (Downers Grove, IL: Inter-Varsity, 2005).

27. Brewin, *Signs of Emergence*, 97.

Interlude Identifying the Streams

1. http://www.pioneer.org.uk/.
2. http://www.ichthus.org.uk/.
3. http://www.revelation.org.uk/.
4. http://JesusCreed.org.
5. Scot McKnight, "Five Streams of the Emerging Chruch," *Christianity Today*, February 2007, 36–39, http://www.ctlibrary .com/ct/2007/february/11.35.html (accessed October 14, 2008).
6. Ibid., 36. McKnight notes James K. A. Smith's *Who's Afraid of Postmodernism?* (Grand Rapids: Baker Academic, 2006) as arguing for postmodernism's compatibility with certain aspects of classical Augustinian epistemology.
7. McKnight, "Five Streams," 37.
8. Ibid., 37–38.
9. Ibid., 38–39.
10. Ibid., 39.
11. Tom Sine, *The New Conspirators* (Downers Grove, IL: InterVarsity, 2008), 24. (For a discussion of each of these categories, see chapter 3.)
12. http://alternativeworship.org.
13. http://NewMonasticism.org.
14. http://emergingpensees.blogspot.com /2006/10/converging-church.html.
15. http://blog.christianitytoday.com/outo fur/archives/2007/03/the_future_of_t.html.
16. Tony Jones, *The New Christians: Dispatches from the Emergent Frontier* (San Francisco: Jossey-Bass, 2008), 8.

Chapter 3 Fresh Expressions

1. David T. Olson, *The American Church in Crisis* (Grand Rapids: Zondervan, 2008), 144–57.
2. *Mission-Shaped Church: Church Planting and Fresh Expressions of Church in a Changing Context* (London: Church House, 2004).
3. http://www.cofe.anglican.org.

4. http://www.cofe.anglican.org/faith/mis sion/missionevangelism.html.
5. "Five Marks of Mission," http://www .cofe.anglican.org/faith/mission/mission evangelism.html.
6. *Mission-Shaped Church*, 81–82.
7. Ibid., xii.
8. Ibid., 7.
9. Ibid., 21.
10. Ibid., 27.
11. http://freshexpressions.org.uk/section .asp?id=3102 (accessed August 16, 2008).
12. http://www.prospects.org.uk/. Causeway Prospects operates internationally, including in the United Kingdom.
13. The Web site of Fenland Community Church is http://www.fcc.uk.net.
14. *Mission-Shaped Church*, 34.
15. Go to www.freshexpressions.org.uk for further information on this as well as other related resources.
16. Christian Research, *Quadrant*, May 2008, www.christian-research.org.uk.
17. http://www.hope08.com/.
18. http://www.churcharmy.org.uk/ms/sc/ sfc_home.asp.
19. http://www.acpi.org.uk/Joomla/ (accessed July 17, 2008).
20. http://www.churchplantingcanada .ca/.
21. See Craig A. Carter, *Rethinking Christ and Culture: A Post-Christendom Perspective* (Grand Rapids: Brazos, 2006), which provides a thought-provoking critique of H. Richard Niebuhr's classic text, *Christ and Culture*, challenging its accommodation to Christendom. Carter believes we need to rethink the nature of the gospel in a post-Christendom world. It may shake us out of our habit focus and prejudice focus to see Jesus and his radical message of the kingdom in a new light.
22. http://www.apostleschurch.org/home .php.
23. "Church of the Apostles, Seattle," *The Lutheran*, June 2006, http://findarticles. com/p/articles/mi_qa3942/is_200606/ai_ n17182791 (accessed August 15, 2008).

24. http://www.fremontabbey.org/about
.html (accessed August 15, 2008).

25. http://www.reformergent.org/?p=20.

26. Adam Walker Cleaveland, "Can Presbymergent Save the PC(USA)?" December 21,
2007, http://pomomusings.com/2007/11/21/
can-presbymergent-save-the-pcusa/.

27. "PC(USA) Awards Grants to Two Presbymergent Communities," December 10,
2007, http://presbymergent.org/ 2007/12/10/
pcusa-awards-grants-to-two-presbymergent
-communities/.

28. David T. Olson, personal e-mail, January 29, 2009.

29. http://www.nabconference.org/pages
.asp?pageid=713#top.

30. http://www.anglican-church-planting
.org/.

31. http://www.mvnu.edu/churchrelations/
faq.asp (accessed July 31, 2008).

32. Tim Keel, *Intuitive Leadership* (Grand
Rapids: Baker, 2007), 83.

33. http://jacobswellchurch.org/.

34. http://jacobswellchurch.org/story (emphasis original).

35. Ibid.

36. Deiter Zander provides a brief account
of his story in Eddie Gibbs and Ryan K.
Bolger, *Emerging Churches* (Grand Rapids:
Baker; London: SPCK, 2005), 323–28. See
also http://newsongsd.org/253217.ihtml (accessed January 29, 2009).

37. Gibbs and Bolger, *Emerging Churches*,
324.

38. http://newsongsd.org/253217.ihtml.

39. Gibbs and Bolger, *Emerging Churches*,
327. See the Web site of ReIMAGINE!, http://
www.reimagine.org/node/1.

40. http://www.baymarin.org/aboutBM/
staff.htm.

41. http://www.solomonsporch.com/.

42. http://www.marshill.org/believe/direc
tions/.

43. http://vfc.tech-wanderings.com/about/
become/missional.

44. http://www.canadianchristianity.com/
cgi-bin/na.cgi?nationalupdates/031211com
ment2.

45. http://www.southside.ca/index.php
?option=com_content&task=view&id=25&
Itemid=52.

46. http://www.ecclesiax.com/.

Chapter 4 The Megachurch Factor

1. Hartford Institute for Religion Research,
"New Research Debunks 11 Myths About
Megachurches," Source Publications, February 3, 2006, http://www.hartfordinstitute
.org/megachurch/megastoday2005_press
release.html (accessed July 8, 2008).

2. "Rise of Megachurches," *CQ Researcher*
17, no. 33 (September 21, 2007): 769–92. See
also D. Michael Linsey, *Faith in the Halls of
Power* (New York: Oxford University Press,
2007). For an extensive analysis see Scott
Thumma and Dave Travis, *Beyond Megachurch Myths: What We Can Learn from
America's Largest Churches* (San Francisco:
Jossey-Bass, 2007).

3. Hartford Institute for Religion Research,
"New Research Debunks 11 Myths." The authors Scott Thumma and Dave Travis have
elaborated on this research in their book,
Beyond Megachurch Myths.

4. Research conducted by Rich Houseal and
the Nazarene Research Center in 2002 re-
vealed a remarkably similar profile of church
size by attendance across six denominations.
See Bill Sullivan, "Understanding Church
Size Based on Empirical Data," *Journal of
The American Society for Church Growth* 19
(Winter 2008): 13–22.

5. However, there are some insights that
are transferable because they are not dependent on either staffing resources or size of
the church.

6. "U.S. Religious Landscape Survey," Pew
Forum on Religion and Public Life, http://
religions.pewforum.org/ (accessed March
17, 2008).

7. *2005 English Church Census* (London:
Christian Research, 2006). For a fuller discussion, see Peter Brierley, *Pulling Out of
the Nosedive* (London: Christian Research,
2006).

8. The increasing significance of ministry to seniors must not be overlooked, however. As Boomers pass into this age category, they will represent a significant swelling of the ranks. They will be more active than previous generations, with a longer life expectancy.

9. David F. Wells, *The Courage to Be Protestant: Truth-Lovers, Marketers and Emergents in the Postmodern World* (Grand Rapids: Eerdmans, 2008).

10. Greg L. Hawkins and Cally Parkinson, *Reveal: Where Are You?* (Barrington, IL: Willow Creek Resources, 2007).

11. Ibid., 31.

12. Ibid., 23.

13. Ibid., 3–4.

14. Ibid., 4.

15. Ibid., 33–35.

16. Ibid., 39.

17. See Albert Hsu, *The Suburban Christian* (Downers Grove, IL: InterVarsity, 2006), and his blog, http://thesuburban christian.blogspot.com/.

18. Hawkins and Parkinson, *Reveal*, 41–43.

19. Bill Donahue, personal e-mail, January 29, 2009.

20. See Brian Sanders, *Life after Church: God's Call to Disillusioned Christians* (Downers Grove, IL: InterVarsity, 2007).

21. Hawkins and Parkinson, *Reveal*, 44–45.

22. Ibid., 45.

23. Ibid., 47.

24. Ibid., 49.

25. Ibid., 53.

26. Ibid., 50.

27. Ibid., 55.

28. Ibid., 65.

29. Compare Thabiti Anyabwile, *What Is a Healthy Church Member?* (Wheaton, IL: Good News/Crossway, 2008).

30. David Fitch, "The WMBI REVEAL Inteview: What I Would Have Said if I Had Had the Chance," Reclaiming the Mission, December 13, 2007, http://www.reclaiming themission.com/.

31. http://www.newurbanism.org. This Web site defines "new urbanism" as "giving more people more choices about how and where they want to live, while providing the solutions to global warming, climate change, and peak oil." NewUrbanism.org was started in 1998 and has since grown to become a leading and well-respected informational Web site promoting good urbanism, smart transportation, transit-oriented development, and sustainability. NewUrbanism.org is independently owned and operated and is not connected to any organization, corporation, or public entity.

32. Hawkins and Parkinson, *Reveal*, 65.

33. Ibid., 65–66.

34. Thumma and Travis, *Beyond Megachurch Myths*, 30–41.

35. Personal e-mail, July 7, 2008.

36. Mike Breen and Walt Kallestad, *The Passionate Church* (Colorado Springs: NexGen/Cook Communications, 2005), 13.

37. Ibid., 23.

38. http://www.joyonline.org/.

39. Daniel Collison, "Growing Wooddale Church in a Post-Christendom World: A Contextual Analysis," unpublished DMin paper, 2007.

40. Wooddale Church Constitution, article 3, revised February 2005.

41. Collison, "Growing Wooddale Church," 7.

42. Information supplied by Peter Brierley in personal correspondence, July 8, 2008. For a more complete list see his *Pulling Out of the Nosedive*, chapter 7, note 22.

43. An interview with Scott Thumma, co-author of *Beyond Megachurch Myths*, reveals that megachurches overall are retaining a high percentage of under-35s: "Based on our research, it is abundantly clear that persons aged 18–35 are not absent from megachurches (nearly 50% of megas report 40% or more of their attendees are under 35 years old—compared to 25% of churches of all sizes in a national study who report this level of young adults in their congregation)" (https://www.theporpoisedivinglife.com, posted September 29, 2007).

44. See Ruth A. Tucker, *Left Behind in a Megachurch World: How God Works through*

Ordinary Churches (Grand Rapids: Baker, 2006).

Chapter 5 Urban Engagement

1. See, for example, http://www.cityona hillmilwaukee.org/content/our-programs -adopt-block.asp (accessed August 1, 2008).
2. http://www.erc.la/.
3. Bill White, "Emmanuel Reformed Church's Journey to Become Missional," unpublished DMin paper, 2007.
4. Alan Roxburgh and Fred Romanuk, *The Missional Leader: Equipping Your Church to Reach a Changing World* (San Francisco: Jossey-Bass, 2006), xv.
5. White, "Emmanuel Reformed Church's Journey," 4.
6. Ibid., 13.
7. Ibid., 7.
8. Ibid., 12.
9. Ibid., 6.
10. http://www.gcbchurch.ca/about/vision .html.
11. For an insider's account of the Eden Project see Matt Wilson, *Eden: Called to the Streets* (Eastbourne, UK: Survivor/Kingsway, 2005), which describes how the prayer emphasis is foundational to the project. See also Debra and Frank Green, *City Changing Prayer* (Eastbourne, UK: Survivor/Kingsway, 2005).
12. http://www.manchester2002-uk.com/ districts/wythenshawe.html.
13. See Eddie Gibbs, *Winning Them Back: Tackling the Problem of Nominal Christianity* (Tunbridge Wells, UK: Monarch, 1993), 125–28.
14. Cameron Dante, *Ascension* (San Francisco: HarperCollins, 2001).
15. http://www.crossrhythms.co.uk/ articles/newsThe_Tribe_Bow_Out/12924/ p1/.
16. http://www.message.org.uk/press .cfm?&ID=299.
17. http://www.message.org.uk/edenproj ect.cfm.

18. Ibid.
19. http://www.message.org.uk/press.cfm ?&ID=299.
20. Ibid.
21. Ibid.
22. Ibid.
23. http://www.message.org.uk/press.cfm ?&ID=298 (accessed March 11, 2008).
24. The Prince of Wales, "A Speech by HRH The Prince of Wales at a reception for Hope 2008 volunteers, Clarence House, London," June 11, 2008, http://www.princeofwales.gov .uk/speechesandarticles/a_speech_by_hrh_ the_prince_of_wales_at_a_reception_for_ hope__756366988.html.
25. http://www.hope08.com/Publisher/ Article.aspx?ID=80291 (accessed July 21, 2008).
26. Bob Hopkins and Mike Breen, *Clusters: Creative Mid-Sized Missional Communities* (3 Dimension Ministries, 2007), www.3dministries.com.
27. Ibid., 34.
28. See Ibid., especially chapter 3, "The Three Dimensions of Clusters," 55–64.
29. Ibid., 41
30. Ibid., 45.
31. Mike Breen and Walt Kallestad, *The Passionate Church* (Colorado Springs: NexGen/Cook Communications, 2005), in which a chapter is devoted to each of the LifeShapes.
32. http://www.3dministries.com/chu rch/contentphp?section_id=21& commun ity_type_id=1.
33. See George Barna, *Revolution* (Wheaton, IL: Tyndale, 2005); Neil Cole, *Organic Church* (San Francisco: Jossey-Bass, 2005); and Thom S. Rainer and Eric Geiger, *Simple Church* (Nashville: Broadman, 2006).
34. Hopkins and Breen, *Clusters*, 35.
35. http://www.st-andrews.org.uk/.
36. http://www.soulsurvivor.com/.
37. Information supplied by Peter Brierley, personal correspondence, June 24, 2008. See also http://trinitycheltenham.com/.
38. Randy Frazee, *The Connecting Church: Beyond Small Groups to Authentic Commu-*

nity (Grand Rapids: Zondervan, 2001), 21, 22 (italics original).

39. http://trinitygracechurch.com/.

40. Tom Sine, *The New Conspirators* (Downers Grove, IL: InterVarsity, 2008), 45.

41 Tommy Kyllonen, *Un.orthodox: Church, Hip-Hop, Culture* (Grand Rapids: Zondervan, 2007), 180.

42. http://www.pbs.org/wnet/religionand ethics/week825/cover.html.

43. http://www.hiphopchurch.org/index2 .html; see also http://www.luke418.org/.

44. http://lawndalechurch.org/.

45. http://lawndalechurch.org/bio.html.

46. http://lawndalechurch.org/index.html.

47. http://www.gloriousundead.com/.

48. http://www.seattlequest.org/.

49. http://www.qcafe.org/about-q-cafe (accessed January 30, 2009).

50. Ibid.

51. http://mosaic.org/about/.

52. http://www.mosaicalliance.com/.

53. David T. Olson, personal e-mail, January 31, 2009.

54. http://www.crmleaders.org/.

55. http://www.crmleaders.org/ministries/ usministries/iteams/urban-mosaic (accessed July 22, 2008).

56. http://www.intervarsity.org/urban/ (accessed July 22, 2008).

57. http://www.worldimpact.org/about/ index.php.

58. A more comprehensive list of urban ministries is available online at http://dir .yahoo.com/Society_and_Culture/Religion _and_Spirituality/Faiths_and_Practices/Chr istianity/Organizations/Urban_Ministries/ (accessed July 22, 2008).

Chapter 6 Resurgent Monasticism

1. Tom Sine, *The New Conspirators* (Downers Grove, IL: InterVarsity, 2008), 49.

2. Jonathan Wilson-Hartgrove, *New Monasticism: What It Has to Say to Today's Church* (Grand Rapids: Brazos, 2008), 21.

3. Ibid., 19.

4. See Jonathan Wilson, *Living Faithfully in a Fragmented World: Lessons for the Church from MacIntyre's* After Virtue (Harrisburg, PA: Trinity, 1997).

5. http://www.newmonasticism.org/12 marks/ (accessed January 14, 2008) and Wilson-Hartgrove, *New Monasticism*, 80.

6. Wilson-Hartgrove, *New Monasticism*, 86.

7. http://www.kanaan.org/international/ default.htm (accessed November 4, 2008).

8. http://www.kanaan.org/international/ sisterhood/default.htm (accessed November 4, 2008).

9. http://www.taize.fr/en (accessed January 14, 2008).

10. http://www.iona.org.uk/.

11. http://www.iona.org.uk/abbey_home .php.

12. http://www.iona.org.uk/iona_commun ity.php.

13. http://www.icmi.org/.

14. http://www.missio-dei.com/rule/.

15. http://www.abbeyway.org/affiliation/.

16. http://www.abbeyway.org/practices/ (accessed January 29, 2008).

17. http://www.abbeyway.org/principles/ (accessed January 29, 2008).

18. http://www.servantsasia.org/index.php/ canada (accessed January 16, 2008).

19. http://rebaplacefellowship.org/ (accessed January 14, 2008).

20. http://www.livingstonemonastery.org/ (accessed February 2, 2009).

21. http://www.newjerusalemnow.org/ home.htm (accessed January 12, 2008).

22. http://directory.ic.org/records/?action =view&page=view&record_id= 21345.

23. For information about each of the Life-Shapes see http://www.3dministries.com/dis cipleship/index-php?Selected Media=3.

24. http://www.missionorder.org/page/ show/62 (accessed January 14, 2008).

25. http://www.missionorder.org/page/ show/65 (accessed January 15, 2008).

26. http://www.missionorder.org/show /76.

27. http://www.missionorder.org/page/ show/69 (accessed January 14, 2008).

28. The draft proposal for the Bishops' Mission Order can be viewed on http://www.freshexpressions.org.uk/section.asp?id=2490 (accessed July 23, 2008).

29. http://www.reclaimingthemission.com/2007/10/missional-order-of-st-fiacre-at-life-on-the-vine.html (accessed March 12, 2008).

30. http://www.worldvision.org/.

31. http://www.tearfund.org/.

32. http://www.tearfund.org/About+us/Tearcraft/ (accessed July 23, 2008).

33. http://www.missionyear.org.

34. http://www.crmleaders.org/minis tries/innerchange/inside-innerchange.

35. http://crmleaders.org/ministries/innerchange (accessed February 2, 2009).

Chapter 7 Expanding Networks

1. http://www.calvarychapel.com/.

2. For a more in-depth study of "apostles," see Francis H. Agnew, "The Origin of the NT Apostle-Concept: A Review of Research," *Journal of Biblical Literature* 105 (1986): 75–96; James D. G. Dunn, *Christianity in the Making*, vol. 1, *Jesus Remembered* (Grand Rapids: Eerdmans, 2003); J. Andrew Kirk, "Apostleship since Rengstorf: Towards a Synthesis," *New Testament Studies* 21 (1974–75): 249–64; John P. Meier, *A Marginal Jew*, vol. 3, *Companions and Competitors* (New York: Doubleday, 2001); Eckhard Schnabel, *Early Christian Mission*, vol. 1, *Jesus and the Twelve* (Downers Grove, IL: InterVarsity, 2004); Rudolf Schnackenburg, "Apostles before and during Paul's Time," in *Apostolic History and the Gospel*, ed. W. Ward Gasque and Ralph P. Martin (Grand Rapids: Eerdmans, 1970), 287–303.

3. C. K. Barrett, *The Signs of an Apostle* (Carlisle, UK: Paternoster, 1996), 52–53. Originally published in 1969 by Epworth Press.

4. Martin Garner, *A Call for Apostles Today* (Cambridge, UK: Grove Books, 2007), 16.

5. See C. E. B. Cranfield, *Romans: A Shorter Commentary* (Grand Rapids: Eerdmans, 1985), 377; and J. R. W. Stott, *Romans: God's*

Great News for the World (Downers Grove, IL: InterVarsity, 1994), 396. Both commentators opt for the feminine form.

6. It must be admitted that this is an oversimplification of a complex issue, as the term "apostle" is used in a wider variety of ways in the New Testament. C. K. Barrett distinguishes between at least eight persons, or groups of persons, all denoted, with varying degrees of propriety, by the term "apostle" (*Signs of an Apostle*, 72–74).

7. Garner, *Call for Apostles*, 8.

8. http://www.vineyardusa.org/about/history.aspx (accessed July 24, 2008).

9. http://www.emergent-uk.org/2007/index.htm.

10. http://www.greenbelt.org.uk/?a=811&pr=126&day=&genre=3 (accessed January 24, 2008).

11. http://www.newfrontiers.xtn.org/about-us/history/ (accessed July 23, 2008).

12. http://www.cmaresources.org. A list of the churches and networks that are associated with Church Multiplication Associates can be found at http://cmaresources.org/networks.

13. http://cmaresources.org/greenhouse.

14. http://cmaresources.org/about (accessed February 2, 2009).

15. http://cmaresources.org/about/history.

16. Ibid. (accessed February 2, 2009).

17. Neil Cole, *Organic Church* (San Francisco: Jossey-Bass, 2005), 26.

18. Ibid., 27.

19. http://ecclesianet.com.

20. http://ecclesianet.com/about/vision/ (accessed February 2, 2009).

21. http://ecclesianet.com/about/core-functions/ (accessed February 2, 2009).

22. See the Web site of Artist at the Fountain, http://www.thefountainroom.com.

23. Quoted in Rick Warren, *The Purpose Driven Church* (Grand Rapids: Zondervan, 1995), 82.

24. Geoff Surratt, Greg Ligon, and Warren Bird, *The Multi-Site Church Revolution: Being One Church in Many Locations*, Leadership Network Innovation Series (Grand Rapids: Zondervan, 2006).

25. http://mondaymorninginsight.com/ index.php/site/comments/multi_site_con ference_session_1/.

26. http://www.northcoastchurch.com/ about_us/our_history/.

27. http://www.multisitechurchrevolution .com/.

28. http:/www.fellowshipchurch.com/wel come?FCW=kgqtfg7ilm8ttp284dqi6p21 (accessed February 2, 2009).

29. http://www.fellowshipchurch.com/wel come (accessed February 2, 2009).

30. http://www.seacoast.org/.

31. http://www.hopeingod.org/AboutUs .aspx (accessed January 12, 2008).

32. http://www.hopeingod.org/Preaching Schedule.aspx (accessed January 12, 2008).

33. http://www.marshillchurch.org/about/ history.

34. http://www.redeemer.com/connect/ affiliated_churches.html (accessed January 11, 2008).

35. http://www.redeemer.com/about_us/ church_planting/ (accessed January 11, 2008).

36. http://www.acts29network.org/about /welcome/.

37. http://en.wikipedia.org/wiki/Multi -site_church.

38. http://digital.leadnet.org/2008/10/in side-look-at.html/ (accessed February 2, 2009).

39. http://www.internetchurchcampus .com/ (accessed February 2, 2009).

40. http://www.leadnet.org/LC_Church Planting.asp.

41. Ibid.

42. Ibid.

43. http://www.leadnet.org/news_102920 07.asp (accessed February 2, 2009).

44. See Ed Stetzer and David Putnam, *Breaking the Missional Code: When Churches Become Missionaries in Their Communities* (Nashville: Broadman & Holman, 2008).

45. http://www.stadia.cc.

46. http://www.stadia.cc/who/name.asp.

47. http://www.stadia.cc/what/.

48. http://www.acts29network.org.

49. Collin Hansen, "Young, Restless, Reformed," *Christianity Today*, September 2006, http://www.christianitytoday.com/ct/2006/ september/42.32.html.

50. http://www.desiringgod.org/Events/ NationalConferences/Archives/2006/.

51. http://www.sovereigngraceministries .org/.

52. http://www.sovereigngraceministries .org/Sovereign Grace Ministries[2] (accessed January 12, 2008).

53. http://www.sovereigngraceministries .org/Churches/USMap.aspx (accessed January 12, 2008).

54. http://www.springharvest.org/ (accessed July 29, 2008).

55. http://www.new-wine.org/about_us/ Our%20History.htm (accessed February 2, 2009).

Chapter 8 The Heartbeat of Worship

1. As I type this chapter I am listening to contemporary music settings of the Odes of Solomon, which are dated by most scholars between the first and third centuries (*The Odes Project*, Worship Leader Partnership, http://www.theodesproject.com/faq [accessed August, 19, 2008]).

2. Professor Corcoran posted a report of their visit, along with a description of Alt.Worship, on his Web site ("Pubs, Clubs and Alternative Worship," http://www.calvin .edu/news/interim/blogsandprojects/proj ect2.html [accessed February 2, 2009]).

3. Eddie Gibbs and Ryan K. Bolger, *Emerging Churches* (Grand Rapids: Baker; London: SPCK, 2005).

4. http://www.calvin.edu/news/interim/ blogsandprojects/project2.html (accessed February 2, 2009).

5. http://www.alternativeworship.org/defi nitions_definition.html (accessed January 21, 2008).

6. http://www.calvin.edu/news/interim/ blogsandprojects/project2.html (accessed February 2, 2009).

7. http://www.alternativeworship.org/defi nitions_definition.html

8. A listing of Alt.Worship centers can be found at http://www.alternativeworship.org/ directory_grouplist.html (accessed January 22, 2008).

9. One helpful resource is the Web site maintained by Steve Collins, called "Small-Fire," which provides a photo gallery of a number of alternative worship locations illustrating the range of their creativity (http://www.smallfire.org/). Another site, called "Mootique" and run by Moot in Westminster, London, has a number of useful tools available for those who may be looking to explore alternative worship forms (http://www.moot .uk.net/mootique/).

10. http://www.greenbelt.org.uk/?s=2 (accessed January 22, 2008).

11. http://www.greenbelt.org.uk/.

12. http://www.greenbelt.org.uk/?s=33 (accessed January 22, 2008).

13. http://www.transmissioning.org/ ?page -id=2.

14. http://www.freshworship.org/what is grace.

15. http://www.visions-york.org/visions .html (accessed January 24, 2008).

16. http://www.visions-york.org/spiritual ity.html (accesssed January 24, 2008).

17. http://www.visions-york.org/visions .html.

18. http://www.visions-york.org/spiritual ity.html (accessed January 24, 2008).

19. http://www.sanctus1.co.uk/sanctus1 home.htm (accessed January 24, 2008).

20. http://www.sanctus1.co.uk/sanctus1 nexus.htm (accessed January 24, 2008).

21. http://www.sanctus1.co.uk/sanctus1 whoweare.htm (accessed January 24, 2008).

22. See, for example, http://www.cafechu rch.org.au/; http://www.cafechurch.org/; http://www.believersseekersdoubters.org .uk/events.php.

23. John D. Witvliet, *The Biblical Psalms in Christian Worship* (Grand Rapids: Eerdmans, 2007), xviii.

24. Ibid., 11 (emphasis original).

25. Ibid., 14.

26. Ibid., 18-20.

27. Ibid., 33.

28. See also Psalms 8:1; 22:27; 47:6-7; 66:1, 4; 67:3-4; 72:19; 97:1.

29. 1 Kings 8:41-43; 2 Chronicles 6:32-34; Isaiah 56:7; Mark 11:17.

Appendix: Distinctive Features of Morphing Churches

1. The Gospel and Our Culture Network, "Empirical Indicators of a 'Missional Church,'" *The Gospel and Our Culture* 10, no. 3 (September 1998): 7, http://www.gocn.org/ newsletters/pdf/103-newsletter.pdf (accessed November 14, 2008).

2. Kester Brewin, *Signs of Emergence* (Grand Rapids: Baker, 2007), 97-116.

3. Eddie Gibbs and Ryan K. Bolger, *Emerging Churches* (Grand Rapids: Baker; London: SPCK, 2005), 43-44.

4. Tom Sine, *The New Conspirators* (Downers Grove, IL: InterVarsity, 2008), 39.

5. Tony Jones, *The New Christians: Dispatches from the Emergent Frontier* (San Francisco: Jossey-Bass, 2008).

index

ALLELON
A Movement of Missional Leaders

Allelon's mission is to **educate** and **encourage** the church to become a people among whom God can live, as sign, symbol, and foretaste of his redeeming love and grace in their neighborhoods and the whole of society—ordinary women and men endeavoring to participate in God's mission to reclaim and restore the whole of creation and to bear witness to the world of a new way of being human.

Visit **www.allelon.org** to read current missional thinkers, learn about our projects and resources, and more.

- Video and Audio of Leading Missional Thinkers and Practitioners
- Articles and Conversations
- Allelon Training Centers
- International Research Project: Mission in Western Culture

The word *allelon* is a common but overlooked New Testament word that is reciprocal in nature. Christian faith is not an individual matter. Everything in the life of the church is done *allelon*, for the sake of the world. A Christian community is defined by the *allelon* sayings in Scripture. We are to love one another. We are to pursue one another's good. We are to build up one another. We are to bear with one another in love. We are to bear one another's burdens. We are to be kind to one another. We are to be compassionate to one another. We are to be forgiving to one another. We are to submit to one another. We are to consider one another better than ourselves. We are to be devoted to one another in love. We are to live in harmony with one another.

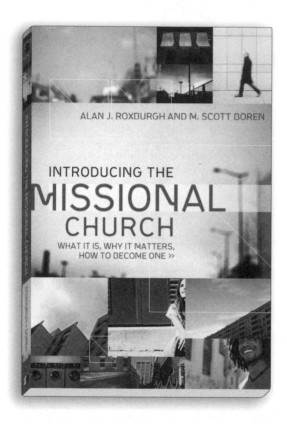

Introducing the Missional Church
WHAT IT IS, WHY IT MATTERS,
HOW TO BECOME ONE

By Alan J. Roxburgh
and M. Scott Boren

9780801072123
208 pp. • $17.99p

Many pastors and church leaders have heard the term "missional" but have only a vague idea of what it means, let alone why it might be important to them. But what does it actually mean? What does a missional church look like and how does it function? Two leading voices in the missional movement here provide an accessible introduction, showing readers how the movement developed, why it is important, and how churches can become more missional.

BakerBooks
a division of Baker Publishing Group
www.BakerBooks.com